Retelling The Story

Creatively Developing Biblical Story Sermons

Larry Lange

CSS Publishing Company, Inc., Lima, Ohio

RETELLING THE STORY

Scripture quotations are from the New Revised Standard Version of the Bible, copyright
1989 by the Division of Christian Education of the National Council of the Churches of
Christ in the USA. Used by permission.

Excerpts from *Celebration and Experience in Preaching* (Nashville: Abingdon Press) by
Henry Mitchell are used by permission.

Excerpts from *Story Journey: An Invitation to the Gospel as Storytelling* (Nashville:
Abingdon Press) by Thomas Boomershine are used by permission.

Excerpts from *Mystery and Manners* (New York: Farrar, Straus & Giroux) by Flannery
O'Connor are used by permission.

Library of Congress Cataloging-in-Publication Data

Lange, Larry.
  Retelling the story : creatively developing biblical story sermons / Larry Lange.
    p. cm.
  ISBN 0-7880-2346-2 (perfect bound : alk. paper)
  1. Story sermons. 2. Preaching. I. Title

BV4307.S7L36 2005
251—dc22

2005002454

For more information about CSS Publishing Company resources, visit our website at
www.csspub.com or e-mail us at custserv@csspub.com or call (800) 241-4056.

ISBN 0-7880-2346-2   PRINTED IN U.S.A.

Table Of Contents

Acknowledgments

I am grateful for the work all the members of my Parish Preaching Groups (PPGs) did during my three years in the Association of Chicago Theological Schools' (ACTS) Doctor of Ministry in Preaching program. I was blessed to have had three different PPGs from four different churches in northeastern Wisconsin. My first PPG was composed of members of Bethel Lutheran Church of rural Gillette, Wisconsin, and Our Redeemer Lutheran Church of rural Suring, Wisconsin: thanks to Marie Bergsbaken, Bonnie Christiansen, Sandy Hansen, Butch Houska, Ben Miller, his stepfather Clark Miller, and Marion Wagner. My second PPG was composed of members from Our Savior Lutheran Church of Lessor Township: thanks to Val Adamski, Zandy Allen, Gary Boerst, Jodi Lawrenz, Arlene Ruechel, and Todd Stiede. A special thanks to Val for her organic, Democratic Party cheese and to Arlene for the line that gave birth to the character of the Widow of Zarephath. Arlene imagined the Widow of Zarephath responding to Elijah's request for food in this way: "Why don't you work for it like the rest of us?"

Now that's a classic!

Finally, I am grateful to the PPG at Grace Lutheran Church of Green Bay, Wisconsin, the congregation with whom I presently serve: thanks to Pam Anderson, Renata Fengler, Audrey Nelson, Ron Pascale, his son Nathaniel, Dick Schiller, and Mildred Watermolen.

Another group of people I am particularly grateful to are those who have risked their personal and professional reputations by "starring" in my off-the-wall, experimental, dramatic sermons over the years. Becky Bunkert and Andrew Birling at Zion Lutheran Church in Appleton were my first collaborators. Those who served in this capacity during my work in the ACTS program were Devon Styczynski (Samuel), Mark Rosen (Hophni, Eli's son), Maddie Holmes (the Widow of Zarephath) and her stepson Philip (the widow's son), Sue Hougard, and Brinda Ruggles. Thank you all! You were all very brave!

I have also been very appreciative of the faculty and my classmates in the ACTS program. It's a rigorous program, the ecumenical nature of which has been greatly enlightening. I always appreciated my advisor's comments all along the way as well as her attention to the design and completion of my thesis: thank you, Connie Kleingartner! A special thank you to Richard Jensen, former dean of the program, who encouraged me to transform my thesis into this more practical form, so that issues related to preaching by telling stories can continue to be part of the homiletical conversation. For the content and title of this book, I am indebted to Professor Jensen's pioneering work. Thank you, Professor Jensen!

I am very grateful to CSS who is publishing this book so it can be a part of the homiletical conversation. I was greatly blessed with an invitation to the Writers' Workshop program of the Evangelical Lutheran Church in America, at which I finished this manuscript. The comments of Ron Pascale, Kathryn Hasselblad Pascale, and my colleagues Julie Wrubbel-Lange and Jen Lapinskas were essential input for what I accomplished at the workshop: thank you all very much!

Finally, the last five years have been particularly busy ones for my family and me because of this project. Thanks to my parents James and Barbara Lange for their help during my weeks away from home in the summer! Preparing for those summer classes, being away from home for those three weeks, completing the parish projects, and rewriting the thesis as a book were an additional workload not only for me, but especially for my spouse, Julie. It's been a great gift for me to have had the chance to pursue the truth and to have found it so efficaciously proclaimed as various forms of fiction. Those who tilt at windmills require the most exceptional of friends. Julie has been that friend, for which I am the most grateful of all.

Introduction

You've come across a biblical story upon which you've preached many times. You're looking for a new approach. You'd like to retell that biblical story in a creative way. But how creative should you be? How do you transform a twenty-verse pericope into a compelling retelling of a biblical story, especially if it's a story many people have already heard many times? Can your creativity twist or obscure or diminish the gospel? It can. Yet if you'd like to preach by retelling biblical stories, a large measure of creativity is essential.

A large measure of creativity is both dangerous and essential when preaching by retelling biblical stories — this theme arose often while I learned to preach this way. This book summarizes some of what I learned as a student in the Doctor of Ministry in Preaching program of the Association of Chicago Theological Schools (ACTS). Originally, I entered this program with two goals in mind: to learn to preach by simply telling stories and to find out how people in the pew experienced these kinds of sermons. Maybe people dislike these kinds of sermons. Maybe they are confused by them. Maybe they are suspicious of them. Maybe these kinds of sermons generate numerous connections between biblical stories and the stories of their own lives. Maybe retelling biblical stories by dramatizing them will become a standard homiletical method taught in seminaries.

Or maybe not.

How will we know the answers to the questions about this unique homiletical method unless we learn about it, unless we go out and preach by retelling biblical stories and then listen carefully to those who hear and see them to learn about their experience of them?

Listening for the experience of the people in the pew is an essential part of the ACTS preaching program. For parish projects during this three-year program, I developed and preached eight sermons for the congregations in which I served. All of these parish project sermons were simply stories — there were no didactic sections in the sermons during which I explained what the stories meant. Five of these sermons retold biblical stories; three were other kinds of story sermons. Three different groups of about seven parishioners and two professors from the ACTS program responded to each of these parish project sermons. Because I was an interim pastor during two of my three years in the program, I worked with three groups of parishioners from four different parishes. The first group was made up of members from both congregations in a two-point parish in rural northern Wisconsin. The second group was made up of members of a small, rural congregation located in an area that is partly a bedroom community for Green Bay, Wisconsin, and partly devoted to dairy farming. The third group was made up of members of the large, downtown congregation in Green Bay at which I presently serve. The members of these groups represent a wonderful diversity of life experiences and occupations. There were farmers, teachers, homemakers, a snowplow operator, a city bus driver, a paper mill worker, a bookkeeper, a florist, a medical lab technician, a high school principal, a college professor, and always at least one high school student. Each group also always represented a good range of ages from those high school students to folks in their seventies.

Despite the great diversity of this group, they all agreed that preaching by retelling biblical stories was a homiletical practice worth pursuing and developing. Experiencing the gospel in a story sermon does not appear to be something only highly educated people can do and enjoy. Oh, the members of my groups had plenty of advice for me! I heard all of their advice as insight into the hearts and minds of members of congregations everywhere. In the pages that follow, you'll hear some of their advice, too. I've been learning the unique craft of preaching by retelling biblical stories with their experiences in mind. You'll also hear from homileticians and writers who have helped me: Robert Alter, Thomas Boomershine, Kevin Bradt, Walter Brueggemann, Frederick Buechner, George Buttrick, Jana Childers, Richard Jensen, Anne Lamott, Eugene Lowry, Henry Mitchell, Flannery O'Connor, Tex Sample, Barbara Brown Taylor, Thomas Troeger, and even the folks at Disney studios! In each chapter of this book, you'll first hear these folks weigh in on a topic germane to preaching by retelling biblical stories; then each chapter (except the first) concludes with one of my sermons to illustrate the issue discussed. Since the first chapter addresses the basic process of developing sermons that retell biblical stories, it includes a sample sermon followed by more comments on the process and from the preaching group.

You're not feeling particularly creative today? You're worried about what members of your congregation will think when you show up Sunday morning and just simply *retell* a biblical story — no explanations, no helpfully organized logical points? That's cool. I've been there and, to a certain extent, I'm still there every week I preach. Despite forty years of books on preaching by telling stories, to judge by the sermons I hear, it's still a new and challenging method for most of us preachers. What follows will introduce you to a friendly, helpful group of traveling companions who are eager to help us retell that old, old story in some very new ways.

Chapter 1

Abandon Truth
All Ye Who Enter Here

Developing A Sermon Which Retells A Biblical Story

Biblical stories were obviously composed in a cultural context radically different from the context of the twenty-first-century people to whom you preach. If you want to preach by retelling biblical stories, you'll need to find a way to explain or interpret a biblical story to make the gospel in it clear. How do you *add* explanation or interpretation to a story without diminishing the dramatic impact of the story? Maybe you can remember a time when you felt let down when a preacher started a sermon by telling a story, but then abruptly turned away from telling a story to explaining or interpreting it. You *can* be creative and *add* basic elements of stories (characters, dialogue, plot) to a biblical story to try to explain and interpret it, but the very idea of *adding* characters, dialogue, or plot to a biblical story tends to raise an eyebrow or two among homileticians and people in the pew. Wouldn't you be abandoning the truth by adding things to a biblical story?

I recall an encounter with the committee whose task it was to certify me for ordination. In the paper I wrote for the committee, I contended that the best homiletical form for conveying the truth of the gospel is a story. When I met with the committee, I learned that several professors on the committee didn't share my high hopes for this notion. The meeting was not going well. Four years of seminary education, four years of *my life* were on the line. Maybe the committee was fidgeting about the amount of creativity storytelling demands. Exasperated, one of the professors finally asked me, "Isn't the truth enough?"

I said, "No."

My stubbornness earned me the assignment of rewriting my paper and another delightful chat with the committee. Still, I stuck to my story.

When preaching by retelling biblical stories, not only is telling the truth not enough; in a way, strictly telling the truth is impossible! In order to preach by retelling biblical stories, biblical stories *do* have to be explained and interpreted by *rewriting* them, by *adding* new characters, dialogue, and/or actions. When preaching by retelling biblical stories, the stories you tell that bear the truth need to be *fabricated!* To me, that's a delightful irony, although I don't think it was for the members of my ordination review committee. They were quite anxious that I was planning to go out into the world to tell idle tales.

Nothing could be further from the truth.

The tales I tell are always informed by the biblical text. Here's a story of one example of how the biblical text guides me as I fabricate stories to retell as sermons that still tell the truth.

Frequently Asking Questions

When you encounter a pericope for the first time, it usually raises more questions than it answers. If you encounter a pericope you've studied for years, it may appear to you that your study of the commentaries has already answered all of your questions about it and some questions you never thought to ask! Now you could certainly support your favorite book publisher and buy some new commentaries, but you could also recruit a group of people from your congregation(s) who *haven't* read all the commentaries and who will invariably have a hundred wonderful questions for you, some of which I guarantee you *won't* be able to answer. For my Doctor of Ministry parish projects, I had to gather preaching groups for just this purpose. It's truly an interesting process, something to try if you feel like you're in a homiletical rut.

For the sermon under consideration, the preaching group had read all the lessons appointed for the Second Sunday After Epiphany (Revised Common Lectionary, Cycle B) including 1 Samuel 3:1-20. We reviewed each passage focusing on the following three questions which are based on a Bible study that accompanies David Rhoads' book, *The Challenge of Diversity.*[1] The three questions are: 1) What do the stories/lessons say about human beings? What are we like? 2) What do the stories/lessons say about God's will for human beings? How does God want us to live? 3) According to the stories/lessons, how does God inspire human beings to live the way he wants them to live? How does God transform us?

The members of the preaching group focused much of their attention on the story in 1 Samuel. This is the story about how Samuel heard the Lord for the first time. What Samuel heard was the disconcerting news that the Lord was not happy with his mentor Eli, because Eli's sons had grown up to be blasphemers. Questions from the preaching group abounded, particularly questions about *why* Eli's sons turned out the way they did.

I learned two things from these questions. One: when I returned home to search for answers to these questions, I learned that the narrator of 1 Samuel didn't seem very interested in answering them. The narrator seemed satisfied with what he considered to be the Lord's statement on this matter: "... [Eli's] sons were blaspheming God, and he did not restrain them" (1 Samuel 3:13). I noticed, in fact, that the narrator of 1 Samuel was interested in other matters in the story of Eli and Samuel. Sometimes creative questions can lead you astray from the concerns of the text. If *you* supply answers to such questions, your answers may have nothing to do with the focus of the text. Based on this experience, I made it a homiletical rule for myself not to attempt to answer questions that are not answered by the text.

As I looked around in vain for answers to the creative questions of my preaching group, I learned a second crucial thing about developing sermons that retell biblical stories. In the process of deciding that the narrator of 1 Samuel wasn't interested in many of the questions my preaching group asked, I had gathered a wonderful record of every detail I could find about Eli and his sons. In this search I was reminded how vital it is to understand the context of a pericope. It's vital not only for understanding the pericope itself, but vital to the fabrication of a new story that *surrounds* and includes the pericope and vital to making sure the new story bears a truth about the old one. And by the way, when is the last time you preached on Sunday for less than five minutes? That's about how long it takes to read most pericopes that are stories. If you preach by simply retelling a biblical story, you *will* need to add

13

things to biblical stories to make the sermon long enough for those who fondly remember the half hour sermons of the good old days.

The Character Of The Characters

I came away from the text and the meeting of the preaching group with a few questions of my own: why was the first message Samuel had to relay as a prophet such a grim one? And why did young Samuel have to give such bad news to his mentor, someone who had apparently taken great delight in Samuel? The members of the preaching group wondered about Eli's failure as a parent. I wondered what the story is saying about the difficulty of telling the truth about others' failures. I wondered to what extent the story of Eli is a story about failure in general or failure in God's sight. I thought failure would be a good theme to explore in this sermon, because feelings of failure lurk in every heart. In the rural context I was serving, failure seemed to be a recurring tragic theme. As we talked about Eli's failure as a parent, the members of the preaching group told me many stories about people who felt they were failing as spouses, as family farmers, as employees, and as parents. The members of the preaching group even felt their churches were failing: membership, attendance, participation, and offerings had been steadily dropping for decades. With *these* questions and realities about failure in mind, I continued biblical study in earnest, prepared, of course, to abandon these questions if it appeared that the narrator of the story of Eli had no interest in them.

Below is that list of all the verses I found necessary for interpreting Eli's character and story.[2]

1 Samuel 1:12-17 — Eli sees Hannah's anguish over her inability to bear a son and rashly accuses her of being drunk. After Hannah's explanation, Eli is equally quick to wish her well, saying, "the God of Israel grant the petition you have made to him."

1 Samuel 2:12-17 — A description of the way Eli's sons treat God's offerings with contempt.

1 Samuel 2:20 — Eli seems particularly grateful for the chance to be Samuel's mentor.

1 Samuel 2:22-25 — Eli is very old. He has not seen any indication that his sons are cavorting "with the women who served at the entrance to the tent of meeting," though he has heard about it. Eli is portrayed as inept and ineffectual both as a priest and as a father. Considering how grateful Eli is for Samuel in 1 Samuel 2:20, it's plausible to imagine the narrator wants us to think Eli regards Samuel as his son, as an opportunity for a second chance to get parenting right or as a chance to "redeem himself." Later, Eli does in fact refer to Samuel as his son (1 Samuel 3:16).

1 Samuel 2:27-36 — A "man of God" addresses Eli. He asks Eli why he has "a greedy eye" for God's sacrifices and offerings, and why he honors his sons more than God by "fattening yourselves on the choicest parts of every offering of my people Israel" (1 Samuel 2:29).[3] Apparently Eli not only allows his sons to sin against the Lord but also participates in their blasphemous feasts.

1 Samuel 3:1-21 — Eli is now Samuel's mentor. Old greedy-eyed Eli's sight has become dim. Eli correctly perceives that it's the Lord who is calling Samuel. After Samuel receives the bad news about God's promise of doom for his family, he is afraid to tell Eli. This indicates that Samuel doesn't think Eli knows about this information. Apparently Eli has kept it a secret from Samuel. Apparently Eli has been concerned that Samuel regards him as an exemplary model of the priestly life. Samuel's hesitation may also indicate that Samuel is afraid that Eli will react strongly to the news. One learns to expect such reactions by experience. Eli's quick, judgmental response to Hannah and Samuel's fear invites readers to understand Eli to be a quick-tempered, emotional man. Eli appears to accept Samuel's announcement of his punishment calmly, although Eli may have said the simple sentence "It is the Lord" in at least two different ways: graciously or begrudgingly.[4]

1 Samuel 4:12-17 — Eli awaits the outcome of an attack of the Philistines on Israel. He is particularly worried about the Ark of the Covenant — not the safety of his sons who had gone off to fight the Philistines. Eli calls a nameless messenger his son: apparently *everyone* is Eli's son ... except his real sons. Robert Alter, in his book *The Art of Biblical Narrative,* teaches us to pay close attention to the "epithets" Old Testament writers use to describe characters.[5] When the capture of the Ark and the death of Eli's sons is reported to Eli, he falls off "his seat by the road," breaks his neck, and dies. The narrator informs us that Eli's death is due to the loss of the Ark, not to the death his sons. These details invite us to understand that Eli no longer honors his sons more than God. Something in Eli seems to have changed since chapters 2 and 3.

1 Samuel 4:12-17 — The narrator also tells us Eli dies when he falls, because he was "an old man and heavy" (1 Samuel 4:18). Is this one of those dark, comic death scenes like the death of Ehud or Sisera? (Judges 3:15-30; 4:1-24). Because the narrator tells us Eli's weight is a factor in his death, does the narrator want us to think of Eli's death as a result of his "greedy eye" for all those nice, roasted offerings he gobbled up or as pious shock or, ironically, as both? The reader has learned to expect Eli to be concerned about his sons. That he is not concerned about his sons, indicates to me that Eli has changed from someone who has indulged himself and honored his sons more than the Lord into someone who now honors the Lord. On the basis of this analysis of Eli's story, I think Eli changes at some point in or between 1 Samuel 3:1-20 and 4:12-18. Many commentators, however, do not consider Eli as "wicked," "corrupt or unfaithful" as his sons — just a lousy parent.[6] If Eli is not "wicked" at the beginning of the biblical story, there is no justification for retelling his story as a story of a radical change of heart at the end of it. Other commentators do offer details that support my interpretation, but they don't articulate an interpretation that covers Eli's whole story.[7] Because retelling Eli's story has forced me to focus on the *whole* story, I have seen how the details of the whole story indict Eli. The narrator does not seem to think Eli was just inept. Eli was as bad as his sons, except at the end of his life. Somehow, Eli had changed. I read this as an ironic story about a guy who finally straightens his life out, but then his pious shock and the consequences of lifelong sinfulness kill him. Maybe the consequences of our failures before God do weigh upon us as long as we live.

Show Or Tell?

Based on this examination of Eli's story, I thought it plausible to characterize Eli as a self-indulgent, inept, emotional man who is concerned with appearances, who is unable to face or confess the truth about himself, and who has, until the very end of his life, indulged himself and his sons' sinful behavior. It has been often noted how seldom biblical narrators tell readers about the inner workings of the human mind.[8] This point is often made to discourage preachers from doing what I've just done: drawing a plausible psychological portrait of a biblical character. Just because biblical narrators don't *tell* us about the inner workings of a character's mind, doesn't mean they aren't interested in readers coming to understand the inner workings of a character's mind. Alter thinks that the actions and dialogue biblical narrators attribute to characters *invite* readers to understand the "moral-psychological depth" of "each fictional situation."[9] Biblical narrators *show* us the inner workings of the human mind without "the imposition of an obtrusive apparatus of authorial interpretation and judgment" so each character can "manifest or reveal himself or herself."[10] Even if the narrators do not *tell* us their point of view about the psychological aspects of a biblical character, they *show* us enough about those characters to invite us to ponder the psychological implications of those actions. Biblical narrators *are* precise about what actions and dialogue they choose to share with us so we *can* summarize what they show us about Eli's character. Making these kinds of summaries is the essential first step in developing characters for your own sermons that retell biblical stories. Then, even if you do add a line of dialogue for Eli to say that doesn't occur in the biblical story, it can still be consistent with Eli's character as presented by the biblical narrator. This sort of careful study of the character of biblical characters justifies, grounds, and guides the process of adding things to a biblical story to retell it as a sermon.

Having a strong impression of Eli's character in mind to help me write every line I had to fabricate for a new story about Eli, I turned my attention to developing a story that utilized the elements of Eli's character and story, a story that seemed to me to be an anatomy of failure, a truth about sin and repentance.

Seven Commandments Of Storytelling
I had developed a thorough, text-based understanding of the character of Eli. I had an idea about the purpose of Eli's story. One

other thing guides me in the process of creating a new story, a story that can serve as a sermon. I had shared with my preaching group a list of vital characteristics of stories and dramas that I had developed with the help of Ted Schroeder, a leader of a writing workshop hosted by my denomination. These are listed below. My new rule guarding against answering questions not raised by the text became "Rule 4."

Rule 1 — Effective stories and dramas attempt to portray real, "round" character(s) dealing with a real challenge or conflict that catalyzes a realistic change in the character(s) in the course of the story or drama.[11]

Rule 2 — These real challenges or conflicts must grow quickly out of character(s) to whom the listener/viewer can quickly respond in either positive or negative ways.

Rule 3 — Dialogue must sound real. Real people do not speak in long monologues nor do they use theological jargon except, for some inscrutable reason, within the confines of seminary classrooms. In sermons, long monologues packed with theological jargon begin to draw attention to themselves; they can quickly appear to listeners to be vehicles for the preacher's agenda; the preacher's intent can become transparent. A listener/viewer's focus can switch from engagement with a character as a real person to whether they agree or disagree with the preacher's opinions. More on "transparent intent" in chapter 5.

Rule 4 — The story or drama should be a plausible interpretation of the text. Don't attempt to answer questions not raised by the text.

Rule 5 — Avoid making references to or assumptions about biblical concepts or stories that people unfamiliar with the Christian faith and scriptures will not understand.

Rule 6 — For dramas, all props, actions, movement, and costumes should be kept simple. Design them with symbolic intentions in mind.[12]

Rule 7 — For dramas, if there's not a lot of time for preparation, designing the production to enable the participants to use a script is a good idea. Still, sometimes it's as much of a problem for people to read effectively from a script as it is for them to memorize one.

I will have reason to refer to these "commandments" occasionally over the course of our time together. I'm still looking for three more, so that it will appear that Moses himself brought them down from Mount Sinai.

As a way of observing the Rules 1 and 2, a member of the preaching group named Butch suggested that the story begin in the midst of a squabble between Eli and his sons. This idea was an excellent one since it allowed me to quickly introduce characters, conflict, and background. (After I had preached the sermon, I publicly thanked Butch for his contribution.) I began to imagine different kinds of disputes that might occur between a father and his unruly sons. The first thing to come to mind was the stock comic situation of a teenager asking to borrow the car. I am well aware that such anachronisms are irritating to some listeners/viewers. Like any aspect of a preacher's style, overuse can draw attention to anachronisms and to the clever preacher who thinks them all up. Most folks tell me, however, that occasional anachronisms function for them as playful and helpful invitations into biblical stories. People genuinely do want to love and respect the scriptures, but for years I have heard quiet complaints about how intimidating and frustrating biblical stories can be. Occasional anachronisms can break the ice, can show listeners/viewers that the people in the Bible are not so very different from us after all.

So Eli's boys need the keys to the camel.

So began the new story. Now obviously there's no story in scriptures about Eli's sons asking to borrow the keys to the camel! How did people react to this obvious attempt to tamper with the truth? None of the members of the preaching group raised any concerns about the use of this anachronistic stock comic situation, nor did they hear any concerns about it from other members of the tightly knit, small congregations in which the sermon was preached. A member of my second preaching group raised more serious issues about attempts to embellish the truth. More on this in chapter 4.

Let's use a different metaphor for the process of developing a sermon that retells a biblical story. Fabrication is associated with processes too mechanical to account for what happens next. Let's use particle acceleration. I began introducing all the elements of Eli's story that I have described above in the particle accelerator of my imagination, and immediately they they began to collide and new discoveries, even new matter began to appear. As new matter has surprised particle physicists by seeming to appear out of nothing, unexpected things happened as I wrote this sermon. A new story of the truth was created, and new connections to the truth happened in the hearts and minds of the people of two small rural congregations in northern Wisconsin. After you have read this new true story of Eli and Samuel, I'll describe the process of writing the sermon and some of the unexpected things that happened along the way.

* * *

My Three Sons
A Sermon for the Second Sunday After Epiphany
(Revised Common Lectionary, Cycle B)
based on 1 Samuel 3:1-20
preached at Bethel and Our Redeemer Lutheran Churches,
Gillette and Suring, Wisconsin

(Eli is seated at a table, center stage. The table contains the remains of Eli's sumptuous dinner. Eli is asleep; his head is resting in his arms that are folded on the table. Hophni, one of Eli's sons, enters from the left.)

Hophni: Hey! Old man! Wake up! Wake up! We need the keys to the camel! *(shakes Eli a bit, but then begins running around, looking for the keys)*

Eli: *(groggy)* What? Awake? Keys? *(shakes head vigorously)* Who goes there?

Hophni: It's me. Hophni. Your beloved son. I need the keys to the camel. Me and Phinehas need to pick up some ladies tonight. So where's the keys, Pops?

(Eli struggles to his feet, tries pathetically to follow Hophni's quick movements. Because Eli is heavy, old, and nearly blind, he can't keep up.)

Eli: You can't have the keys! I'll not be party to your shenanigans, young man! You know how I feel about your behavior! You boys are walking on thin ice!

Hophni: *(finds keys; they jingle as he picks them up)* Cool! *(jingles them in front of Eli's face)*

Eli: *(grasping for the keys)* Give me those keys!

Hophni: Hey. Don't worry, Pops. Don't you think we know we gotta be discrete? We know the *National Enquirer*'s out there snoopin' around. We know that. We may be bad, but we're not stupid! We sneak the girls out, get on the camels outside of town; then it's "Midnight at the Oasis!" And nobody'll know a thing about it.

Eli: *(sitting, shaking his head)* Everybody knows. And God knows. He's told me so. It's over, Hophni. God's promise to allow our family to serve here in the Lord's house is done. God's changed his mind. All the members of our family will die by the sword and you and your brother, Hophni, you're going to die on the same day. And soon! Soon the consequences of this sinful life you lead will catch up to you, to all of us.

Hophni: *(laughing)* Where'd you hear all that stuff, Pops? On the psychic hot line? Pops! This is just a job. And it's an important job, so it has its perks: like plenty to eat and a staff that can't be beat. So we fraternize with them a little. So what? Keeps us all happy. What more is there to life, Pops? Look at you. *(pats Eli on* *the belly)* You've certainly benefited from your position, taking all the best cuts of meat before it gets boiled up in the offering. People don't seem to have a big problem with that. *They* understand that a job like this has its benefits. Well, Phinehas and I aren't interested in *dead* meat, if you know what I mean. We got a life, Pops. We're outta here! *(exits to the left)*

Eli: *(stands, lamely tries to follow, then stops)* Hophni! Hophni!

(Samuel enters from the right. He comes to Eli's side, guides him back to the table, and seats him.)

Samuel: Were you calling for me, Master?

Eli: Ah. It's Samuel. It's you. Thank you, Samuel. Thank you, my son.

Samuel: Master?

Eli: Yes, my son.

Samuel: Why don't you just throw Hophni and Phinehas out? They must be making God angry! And they're ruining your reputation among the people.

Eli: They are my flesh and blood. What will they do if I throw them out? What useful skill did they learn here to help them survive in the real world? Could they farm? Could they herd sheep? They don't know anything about a *real* job. And who'd want them working for them after having been publicly disgraced by being removed as priests? The people believe that God has promised to allow my family to run the Lord's house. If I only dismissed my sons, how would that look to my enemies ... or to their friends? If I dismiss them, I must dismiss myself as well. And then what will *I* do? I don't have any useful skills either! I'd be a disgrace, too. A beggar. I can do nothing, Samuel.

Samuel: Tell the people the truth. Confess your sin before them. And then if Hophni and Phinehas don't repent of *their* sin and stop *their* evil ways, well ... *then* dismiss them.

Eli: Tell the people the truth? Humiliate myself?

Samuel: Everybody knows already.

Eli: *(angry, rising up)* What do they know? What do they know about being a failure in front of God and everybody? What do they know about having their failure parading around in front of them day in and day out? What do they know about God turning his back on me, about God not speaking to me, his priest! What does anybody know about my life? What do *you* know? You're just a boy, just a spoiled little boy who hasn't had to break your back hacking away in the hot sun at an acre of weeds like the rest of the boys your age. What do *you* know? Get out of here! Get out of my sight!

(Samuel runs off.)

Eli: Get out of my sight. What a thing for a blind man to say. Of course, the boy is right. And maybe if I did repent, the Lord would change his mind and wouldn't punish me as he has promised. And maybe those boys'd change, too. Maybe they'd grow up and settle down, and be satisfied with some chops and steaks, and grow jolly and happy like I have, happy enjoying all my blessings. Maybe everything'll turn out all right after all. *(yawns)* I'm so tired. *(begins cleaning up the mess on table)*

Samuel: *(enters from the right)* Here I am, for you called me.

Eli: I did *not* call. Lie down again. *(Eli continues to clean up table. Samuel exits to the right.)* Maybe I shouldn't be so hard on that boy. Yet if I'd been harder on my own boys, maybe they wouldn't be out partying all night long. I never seem to get things right. I never seem to know when to be the tough guy and when to take it easy. I try and I get it wrong. And then God punishes me for it? And then God lets me know about this punishment *second hand*, through some stranger who comes up to me one day out of nowhere and says, "Thus says the Lord. Your family is a bunch a bums." This is what I get for all my years of service here?

Samuel: *(enters from the right)* Here I am, for you called me.

Eli: *(gives Samuel a puzzled look)* I did *not* call, my son! Now, lie down again. *(Samuel exits to the right)* That boy. He's the one thing I've done right. I prayed for his mother who was hated for having no children. I prayed for his mother, and God heard my prayers. And she gave birth to Samuel, the son she always wanted. And then what does *she* do with *her* great blessing? She gives it away. She gave her greatest blessing to me. An amazing woman.

Samuel: *(enters from the right)* Here I am, for you called me.

Eli: *(to congregation)* Again he's here. *(pauses)* I wonder if it's the Lord speaking to him? *(to Samuel)* Go, lie down again, my son; if you hear the voice again, say, "Speak Lord, for your servant is listening." *(Samuel exits to the right — to the congregation again)* It must be the Lord! The Lord speaks to Samuel! Oh, he'll be a great man in Israel! I can just see it! He'll be a comfort to me in my old age. He'll say to all the great men he meets, "Eli is my father. Eli was a good father. Eli is a great man." Yes. Samuel is God's blessing to me to console me and to make me happy. And so it is. And so I can rest at peace.

(Eli seats himself at the table, yawns, stretches, and attempts to fall asleep again at the table in the midst of the mess. Samuel enters from right again. He tiptoes in, sees the mess on Eli's table, and begins cleaning it up. After a while, Eli stirs. Samuel stops, as if fearing punishment.)

Eli: Samuel? Ah, Samuel, my son.

24

Samuel: *(still fearful)* Here I am, Master.

Eli: *(eagerly)* What has the Lord told you? Don't hide it from me. May God do so to you and more if you hide anything from me of all that he told you.

Samuel: *(anxiously)* God said he's about to do something in Israel that will make the ears of anyone who hears it tingle.

Eli: Really! *(to congregation)* Maybe there's hope for me yet. *(to Samuel, eagerly)* What else did the Lord say?

Samuel: *(very anxiously)* The Lord said on that day he will fulfill *against* Eli *(pause)* all that he has spoken concerning Eli's house, from beginning to end.

Eli: *(deflated)* The Lord said that, did he?

Samuel: The Lord said, "For I told Eli ..."

Eli: *(angry, rising)* The Lord told *me* nothing!

Samuel: "... for I told Eli that I am about to punish his house forever for the iniquity he knew, because his sons were blaspheming and he did not restrain them."

Eli: *(desperately trying to save face before Samuel)* I ... I tried to ...

Samuel: *(interrupting ... getting gradually more and more anxious about the message he is delivering)* "Therefore I swear to the house of Eli that the iniquity of Eli's house *shall not be removed* through sacrifices or offerings *(long pause)* forever."

Eli: *(begrudgingly)* It *is* the Lord. Let the Lord do what seems good to him.

Samuel: I'm so sorry, Master. I *had* to tell you.

Eli: I've known it all along, my son. It was revealed to me not by the Lord, but by some stranger, some prophet out of nowhere, some prophet with no credentials, no position like mine. And that's not all. He foretold my sons' deaths. They will die on the same day, and so I wait ... with dread ... for that day.

Hophni: *(enters frantically from the left)* Father, Father, the Ark of the Covenant! We need the Ark of the Covenant! The Philistines are coming up the river valley into the hills to Shiloh! They're attacking all Israel! The army's been defeated once already, Father. They're crying for the Ark! What shall we do?

Eli: *(visibly trying to muster up some enthusiasm)* You and your brother will take them the Ark. We've never been defeated as long as we've had the Ark of the Covenant with us. So you and your brother will save the day.

Hophni: We will? Really? Cool! I'll get Phinehas. *(begins to exit left)* Hey! Phinehas! Phinehas, you lazy bum!

Samuel: *(waits to make sure Hophni is gone)* So this is how they'll die?

Eli: Yes, I can see it already.

Samuel: And you didn't tell them the truth?

Eli: What good is the truth, my son? It's so painful. See how this lie has made them happy? They've lived happily, and now they'll die happily.

Samuel: But maybe if you told them the truth, they'd finally repent, and maybe even now the Lord would change his mind.

Eli: Fat chance. The Lord is dead set against me. You heard yourself. Why take away their happiness with that awful truth?

26

Samuel: But shouldn't the truth be valued for itself, Master, no matter what feelings we have to endure by saying it? I had to tell you the truth about what the Lord said, Master, but I didn't feel like it. I didn't want to make you sad. But the truth must be told.

Eli: I suppose you've spoken wisely, my son, far more wisely than many twice your age. Maybe this is where I've always gone wrong. I've always let my feelings dictate my actions. I loved my sons and so I couldn't tell them the truth that their behavior was wrong. I loved my job, my status, my power, and so I couldn't tell the people the truth about me. By telling the truth, I would've lost everything I loved; and though by living this lie, I *have* kept everything I love. Now, now I'm about to lose it all anyway. I've been selfish, my son, greedy, grabbing on to every blessing that came my way and keeping it for myself.

Samuel: Master, you're being too hard on yourself ...

Eli: I have not been grateful. I don't want you to remember *me*, my son. If there's anyone you should remember it is your mother.

Samuel: My mother?

Eli: Yes. You were her greatest blessing. The very answer to her prayers. And *she* was grateful to the Lord, so grateful that she was inspired to share her greatest blessings for his purposes. She did not hoard all God's blessings for herself as I did. The Lord provided blessings in the midst of her sorrows, because she turned to the Lord and prayed. But now ... *(kneels before Samuel, tugging on his robe)* now what will the Lord give me, what will God give me, now that *I* turn to the Lord in my sorrows?

Samuel: *(tries to back off, regarding Eli's behavior with alarm)* What will the Lord give *you*? You *do* always think only of yourself. I can see that now. *(shakes off Eli's grip)* The Lord has told you what he will give you. You have to suffer the consequences of your sin. Your whole life long. The Lord can surely *forgive* our sin, but the Lord can't always remove its consequences. I have to go to work now. The army needs our prayers. *(Samuel begins to exit to the right)*

Eli: Don't leave me alone, my son!

Samuel: You're not alone, old man. The Lord is with you. It's time you turned to him.

(Samuel exits right — Eli pauses briefly, then speaks the final lines with attention to their sense and not their rhythm and rhyme)

Eli: O Lord God, I have promised, to serve you to the end.
Remain forever near me, my master and my friend.
I shall not fear the battle if you are by my side.
Nor wander from your pathway if you will be my guide.
O let me feel you near me, the world is ever near.
I have seen the sights that dazzle; the tempting sounds I hear.
My foes are ever near me, around me and within.
O please God draw nearer and save my soul from sin.
O let me hear you speaking in accents clear and still
above the storms of passion and murmurs of self-will.
O speak to reassure me, to hasten or control
O speak and make me listen, O guardian of my soul.[13]

Congregation: Sings verse 4 of "O Jesus, I Have Promised"

* * *

The Plot Quickens

As I began creating this imaginary, unbiblical, comical encounter, how Eli acted in this situation was determined by who my biblical study said Eli was. I used the stock comic situation as a new context in which Eli would live and breathe, act and react. I used the new context as a way of conveying background about Eli and his life situation. I used the new context as an introduction to the pericope appointed for the day. Below is a list of critical details that came to be included in my story about Eli and Samuel in order of their appearance along with a brief description of how and why I came to include them.

1. Eli is seated at a table, center. The table contains the remains of a sumptuous dinner. Eli is asleep, his head in his arms that are resting on the table. The first thing the listeners/viewers see when they meet Eli is a picture of the self-indulgent element of his character. This is an example of what is meant by Rule 7: designing props, actions, and costumes with symbolic intentions in mind.

2. Hophni asks for "the keys to the camel" so he and Phinehas can "pick up some ladies." The biblical research is fleshed out with a stock comic situation. Hophni needs the keys to the camel so he and Phinehas can do what the biblical text says they do: "lay with the women who served at the entrance of the tent of meeting" (1 Samuel 2:22). Watching Eli stumble around after Hophni is a simple way to indicate another thing the biblical text tells us: Eli is old, overweight, inept, and nearly blind. Eli has been chasing after his sons ineffectually his whole life long.

3. Hophni reassures Eli that he and Phinehas will be "discreet" because they know "the *National Enquirer*'s out there snoopin' around." This is a reference to the biblical story's report that Hophni and Phinehas have been caught cavorting with "the women who served at the entrance to the tent of meeting" and that people are aware of it.

4. Eli tells Hophni about "the man of God" and his verdict about their family. Presumably Eli had conveyed this information to his sons at some point. Why not here? It serves as background information for the listeners/viewers.

5. True to the biblical accusation that Phinehas and Hophni are blasphemers, Hophni mocks the message of the "man of God." While Eli decries his sons' sins, Hophni is quick to point out Eli's hypocrisy. Eli had gone along with some of his sons' sins: that of appropriating the offering meat for themselves (1 Samuel 2:29). Hophni wonders why Eli begrudges their fraternizing with the female staff members. The people know about all of these scandals and yet have not risen up to remove Eli's family from service. Hophni interprets this as tacit permission from his father and his

society to get away with as much sin as he can. This part of the conversation also serves as background information for the listeners/viewers.

6. When Samuel enters, the listeners/viewers see how grateful Eli is for him. Eli calls Samuel his son, but Samuel corrects Eli so that the listeners/viewers know Samuel is *not* Eli's son but his student. There was some confusion about this and the Ark of the Covenant among the members of my preaching group in the original version of the sermon.[14] This confusion led me to revise the sermon and draft Rule 5: avoid making references to or assumptions about biblical concepts or stories that people unfamiliar with the Christian faith and scriptures will not understand.

The question I wrestled with at this point in the development of the story is this: what should Samuel say to Eli as a prelude to dramatizing the pericope? Samuel is aware that Eli's sons are up to no good. Samuel enters while the old man is pleading with his fleeing son Hophni. It's not a big stretch to imagine Samuel commenting on Eli's sons with youthful idealism, with a young prophet's disdain. Eli's defense of his sons here demonstrates for the listeners/viewers his indulgence of them and some rationalization for it. The preaching group wondered *why* Eli was so indulgent. In offering this speculative rationalization, have I violated Rule 4 about speculating about issues and questions not addressed by the text? These rationalizations developed naturally out of Eli's character and his situation as depicted in the biblical story. I did not develop these rationalizations in order to answer those creative questions my preaching group asked. Had I done so, I could have easily used Eli's character as a way of illustrating one of my favorite twentieth or twenty-first century psychological models of explanations for human behavior. I could have made all kinds of homiletical hay speculating about the reasons for Eli's indulgence of his sons. Was it due to the fact that Eli had had a weak father figure himself? How does the apparently premature death of the boys' mother affect their relationship to their father? To other women? It's easy to see how such speculation could lead a preacher to use the text to illustrate many modern models for explaining human behavior. The biblical story, however, is not an examination of Eli's past; the narrator does not wring his or her hands about how some past psychological trauma has ruined Eli's life and that of his sons. The biblical story is at least partly about Eli's *future*; it's about his potential (or lack thereof) to change, to repent. Yes, I appear to offer a rationalization for Eli's indulgent treatment of his sons. But the rationalization is grounded in Eli's character and story. This rationalization does not impede the momentum of the story. The rationalization for Eli's indulgence here is incidental and not focal. Even though at times it might appear that this distinction is hard to maintain, the distinction is nonetheless there. The distinction is rooted in the *process* of developing these kinds of sermons. As a matter of principle, this process consciously precludes speculation about answers to questions not asked by the text, so that while the preacher is adding new letters to the text, he or she is not violating the spirit of it.

One positive thing the rationalizations provide is a window into Eli's dilemma, a window into which twenty-first-century listeners/viewers can peek to help them understand things about Eli that original readers/hearers of the story could have more easily surmised themselves. Original readers/hearers knew there were very few other viable vocational opportunities available for a disgraced, high-profile religious leader. They would have better understood the enormous level of inescapable public shame associated with such disgrace. Our experience of disgraced religious leaders is that they *can* move to a new community where they can engage in any number of different kinds of occupations in almost complete anonymity.

7. Samuel's youthful idealism runs afoul of Eli. When Samuel suggests that Eli confess his sins, he hits a raw nerve. When the listeners/viewers see Eli turn on Samuel they easily understand later, in the dramatization of the pericope itself, why Samuel is afraid to tell Eli the message of doom for his family. Samuel's suggestions cause Eli to lash out at others around him including God and Samuel. Has Eli really accepted his own sinfulness? Nowhere in the biblical story of Eli, after all, does Eli repent of his implication in his sons' scandals. Nor does the narrator show us that Eli accepts the message from "the man of God." The narrator

of the biblical story rather abruptly turns away from Eli's reaction to "the man of God." To be sure, Eli is not described as throwing "the man of God" out on his ear, but neither does Eli accept the message with repentant sorrow. The narrator simply, abruptly veers away from the episode. This sort of "breaking off of dialogue" may be an example of what Robert Alter calls "an implicit commentary."[15] The narrator includes no response from Eli to imply that from the narrator's point of view there *was* no response, no regret, no repentance on Eli's part.

8. After Eli chases Samuel away, I thought with him for a while about all the things that had gone wrong in his life, and I stumbled on an example of a person in his memory who had *shared* her blessings, who had given them away: Hannah, Samuel's mother. Hannah stands out for the listeners/viewers (*and* in the biblical story) as a contrast to Eli's behavior of trying to cover up his failures in order to hang onto his blessings. Though it's not visible in the brief span of the pericope, there *is* room in this sermon for this contrast that at least one listener/viewer heard very clearly: "I thought one thing that was really good was when [Eli] praised Samuel's mother for being so selfless and to give her only treasure."

9. When Eli discovers that the Lord is speaking to Samuel, true to his unrepentant self, old greedy-eyed Eli fantasizes that the message from the Lord will be about how Samuel will grow up to be famous and will take care of him in his old age. An astute objection was raised by a member in the preaching group named Bonnie about this bit of dialogue added to the pericope: "That's one part that confused me in our little drama here. It sounded like Eli may have somehow believed that this was good news he was going to hear [from Samuel]. Did that come out of the lessons? I missed it ... but we're not to fill in, right?" Am I violating Rule 4 again? Here adding dialogue to the pericope stands out, because it seems to add a new idea to the biblical story. It's not really a new idea at all. It's perfectly consistent with old greedy-eyed Eli for him to be grasping at straws for himself. Immediately again, the listeners/viewers see that Eli is not at all like Hannah. He is the same old self-centered, unrepentant self. Listener/viewer opinion, which at the beginning of the sermon may have pitied Eli, begins

to plummet. Eli falling asleep again in the mess of his meal symbolizes no change in his behavior.

10. When Samuel reluctantly reveals to Eli that his failure will never be "expiated by sacrifice or offering," he negates Eli's self-indulgent fantasies. Because Eli had just been speculating on a comfortable retirement for himself, it would be unrealistic for Eli to suddenly repent at this point. That's why I exploit the potential ambiguity of "It is the Lord." Eli says "It is the Lord" begrudgingly, not with joyful affirmation. It's not until *after* Samuel confronts Eli with his selfish preoccupation and *after* the Lord sets into motion the events that results in the death of his sons that there's a realistic level of dramatic tension necessary for the change that takes place in Eli.

11. The final piece of the plot unexpectedly fell into place as I reached this part of the sermon. I knew that the last chapter of the biblical story involved Eli waiting to hear whether or not the Ark of the Covenant is stolen in a battle with the Philistines. The questions with which I was confronted were: How do I get this battle started? What sort of "last good-bye" would there be for Eli and his sons? Since Eli's sons *were* involved in that battle, it suddenly seemed natural that they would be the ones to appear to inform Eli of the attack of the Philistines. This plan killed two birds, so to speak, with one stone: announcing the battle to the listeners/viewers and getting the sons involved in it. Eli sends them off with a shocking lie that they will save the day and redeem themselves with glorious victory over the Philistines. This must appear appalling to the listeners/viewers. The idea that we can somehow redeem ourselves is discredited. God redeems those who repent. The biblical narrator does not show us Eli's repentance; nor has Eli repented in this sermon — yet. When Eli realizes he really *has* lost everything, true to his selfish character, he wants to know, "What will God give me now?"

12. Samuel confronts Eli's "it's all about me" attitude: "God has told you what he will give you! God can surely forgive our sin, but God can't always remove its consequences." Samuel's remark articulates what the narrator of the biblical story seems to

be saying about Eli's death: though we repent, we do not magically erase all the consequences of our sins. So it is in the biblical story that Eli's death appears to be partly caused by his weight, the consequence of his life-long, greedy-eyed, self-indulgent lifestyle.

13. I chose not to dramatize Eli's death — only the repentance implied in it. Eli dies partly because he is finally more concerned about honoring the Lord (represented by the Ark) than his sons. Samuel articulates the hope that God can forgive Eli, and that God *is* with him. That God is with Eli is the kind of "gospel" statement heard in Psalm 23 or 139 or the kind of gospel that Christians hope in baptism. I found the hymn that Eli quotes at the very end of the sermon by using a liturgical planning resource my denomination publishes. Because of its emphasis on hearing the Lord speak, many other liturgical planning resources probably also recommend this hymn. I was pleasantly surprised to find its words practically perfectly crafted to fit Eli's situation. There is nothing specifically Christian about the first three verses and so they don't appear out of place in the mouth of someone living a thousand years before the time of Jesus. They function as a prayer from Eli for help dealing with his self-indulgence, for help dealing with his mourning over the loss of hearing the Lord's voice, for help dealing with the battle that has just begun with the Philistines, and for help dealing with his need to confess and repent. The congregation joins Eli in singing the last verse, which *is* specifically Christian:

> *O Jesus, you have promised To all who follow you*
> *That where you are in glory Your servant shall be too.*
> *And Jesus, I have promised To serve you to the end;*
> *Oh, give me grace to follow My master and my friend.*
> — *Lutheran Book of Worship*, #503

In this verse, the listeners/viewers bring whatever connection they have made with Eli during the sermon to Jesus. As we sing, we pray, as Eli does, for the grace to follow. Did the listeners/viewers feel a connection with Eli? Bonnie felt a connection: "It really hit home when [Eli was] talking about how strict to be with your children ... you don't know. You don't want to be too hard or too soft; it's something I think of all the time...."

34

Do the listeners/viewers hear good news for their struggles? What follows is a part of the transcript of the meeting at which my preaching group evaluated this sermon.

Bonnie: Can I ask what everyone thinks is the resolution?

Marion: I think the conflict would be Eli's realization of himself.

Bonnie: I think that's the main one. The conflict was not the boys. That was just who they were. The conflict was Eli and God and what he had done with his life. I picked one little passage that pretty well told it to me: "I loved my job, my status, my power, and so I couldn't tell the people the truth about me." What I got out of that was Eli worked for his reward on earth while he should have been working for his reward in heaven. [Eli] realizes his faults — at the end ... It takes God's judgment to wake him up, snap him out of it.

Clark: Actually it takes Samuel's words from God. The way I see the song, [Eli's] asking, but God's still not answering. You can leave us a cliffhanger, too, sometimes, which if you're paying attention, it really makes you think more ... on to more things ... that's somewhat like this: how it made me understand more about Eli.

Marion: "O speak and make me listen ..." I was so pleased when you did that. I knew it was a song when you started it.

Bonnie: I did, too.

Butch: Good finish.

Marion: Really tied it up.

Ben: [God] taught [Eli] a lesson. He taught Eli there are a lot of benefits that come with being a servant. But you can't take advantage of them ...

Marion: Samuel says, "God can surely forgive our sins, but God can't always remove its consequences." I believe that's true. You're *not* alone, old man.

The preaching group experienced the beginning of a change in Eli, a change implied in the first four chapters of 1 Samuel. Some saw aspects of Eli's struggles reflected in their own lives. Even if Clark felt that the sermon left him feeling "God still wasn't answering," the gospel was simply and surely stated by Samuel and remembered by Marion: "You're *not* alone, old man." And, even if Clark didn't hear that and felt the sermon was a "cliff-hanger," he and the congregation sang a prayer for God's help, a prayer affirming God's promises:

> *O Jesus, you have promised To all who follow you*
> *That where you are in glory Your servant shall be too.*
> — *Lutheran Book of Worship*, #503

And even if Clark didn't *sing* to affirm God's promise, God's love and forgiveness were dramatized definitively in the sacrament of Christ's body and blood given and shed for him for the forgiveness of sins. Any kind of sermon can be a "cliffhanger" even if we don't plan it that way. It's vital, therefore, for us to see opportunities throughout the whole service to echo and support the truth in our sermons. Singing hymns that contribute to the meaning of a sermon, or echo the meaning of sermon or that simply conclude a sermon is just one way to accomplish that. More on this topic in chapter 6.

Chapter Notes

1. David Rhoads, *The Challenge of Diversity* (Minneapolis: Fortress Press, 1996), pp. 31-32.

2. For excellent introductions to conducting this kind of literary research, see Robert Alter, *The Art of Biblical Narrative* (New York: Basic Books, 1981); Thomas Boomershine, *Story Journey: An Invitation to the Gospel as Storytelling* (Nashville: Abingdon Press, 1988), pp. 74, 206; Jack Dean Kingsbury, *Matthew as Story* (Philadelphia: Fortress Press, 1986), pp. 9-27, 41-56; David Rhoads and Donald Michie, *Mark as Story* (Philadelphia: Fortress Press, 1982), pp. 101-136.

3. Robert Alter translates it similarly: "why do you trample on My sacrifice and My offering ... and you honor your sons more than Me, to batten upon the first portions of each offering of Israel My people." "Batten" means to become fat and thrive and prosper, especially at another's expense. Richard Alter, *The David Story: A Translation and Commentary of 1 and 2 Samuel* (New York: W. W. Norton and Co. Inc., 1999), p. 14.

4. Ralph David Gehrke, *1 and 2 Samuel*, Concordia Commentary, Walter J. Bartling and Albert E. Glock, eds. (St. Louis: Concordia Publishing House, 1968), pp. 45-46: Gehrke acknowledges the potential ambiguity in Eli's response when Samuel reports the Lord's condemnation of Eli's house, but thinks it more likely that Eli is truly contrite.

5. Alter, *The Art*, pp. 6-7, 122-123, 126-127, 180.

6. Walter Brueggemann, *First and Second Samuel, Interpretation: A Bible Commentary for Teaching and Preaching*, James Luther Mays, ed. (Louisville: John Knox Press, 1990), pp. 23, 26: for Brueggemann, Eli is inept, but not evil.

   P. Kyle McCarter, Jr., *I Samuel,* Anchor Bible, Vol. 8, William Foxwell Albright and David Noel Freedman, eds. (Garden City, New Jersey: Doubleday and Company, Incorporated, 1980), p. 82: McCarter also denies that Eli is wicked.

   William McKane, *I and II Samuel: The Way to the Throne*, Torch Bible Paperbacks, John Marsh and Alan Richardson, eds. (London: SCM Press, Ltd., 1963), p. 46: although McKane notes that Eli threatens Samuel with a curse, Eli nonetheless accepts God's sentence with admirable, pious composure.

7. Alter, *The David Story*, pp. 14, 16, 18, 24: the "man of God" accuses Eli and his sons of "battening" themselves on the offerings — making themselves

fat at the expense of others. Alter also discerns a theme of failing sight in Eli's story: Eli sees Hannah and hastily concludes that she's drunk. He doesn't see his sons cavorting in any way with the temple staff, but hears of it secondhand. In chapter 33, Eli's eyesight is dim; in chapter 4 his eyes are "set" so he could not see at all. Alter thinks this theme parallels and complements a theme of Eli's growing "spiritual" blindness. Alter also reminds the reader that Eli threatens his beloved Samuel with a curse!

Hans Wilhelm Hertzberg, *I and II Samuel: A Commentary*, The Old Testament Library, J. S. Bowden, transl., Peter Ackroyd, James Barr, Bernhard Anderson, James Luther Mays, eds. (Philadelphia: Westminster Press, 1964), pp. 37-38: Hertzberg claims the text is written "to lay special stress" on Eli's responsibility.

Bruce Birch, "I and II Samuel" in the *New Interpreter's Bible*, Vol. 2, Leander Keck et al. eds. (Nashville: Abingdon Press,), p. 988, but then pp. 992-993.

See also Gehrke, pp. 45-46.

8. Alter, *The Art*, pp. 87, 114; Bruce Malina and Richard Rohrbaugh, *Social Science Commentary on the Synoptic Gospels* (Minneapolis: Fortress Press, 1992), p. 231; David Buttrick, *Homiletic* (Philadelphia: Fortress Press, 1987), p. 333.

9. Alter, *The Art*, p. 86.

10. Alter, *The Art*, p. 87.

11. For more information about "round" characters, see Rhoads and Michie, pp. 102-103 and E. M. Forster, *Aspects of the Novel* (New York: Harcourt, Brace, and World, 1927), pp. 65-82.

12. Thomas Troeger, in his book *Ten Strategies for Preaching in a Multi-Media Culture*, also suggests simplicity: "Keep it simple. Do not use any more props or costumes than suggested. Part of why something like this works is its sparseness, the room it allows for the imagination." Keeping things simple can also help highlight themes or messages kinesthetically. You can help define a character by locating certain actions or characters in the same places: the "alienated" character always appears on one side, further away from the center. As the drama goes on, locating "the alienated character" closer and closer to the center can emphasize his or her reconciliation to other characters. See the sample sermon included in this chapter and following chapters 4 and 6 for other examples. Thomas Troeger, *Ten Strategies for Preaching in a Multi-Media Culture* (Nashville: Abingdon Press, 1996), pp. 30-38.

13. "O Jesus, I Have Promised," text John E. Bode in *Lutheran Book of Worship* (Minneapolis and Philadelphia: Augsburg Publishing House and Board of Publications, Lutheran Church in America, 1978), #503.

14. Ben, the high-school-age member of my preaching group, was confused about the Ark of the Covenant. He hadn't heard the term before except in the movie *Raiders of the Lost Ark*. He did not realize the Ark in the movie actually played a part in the Old Testament. Consequently, he was confused and distracted as he tried to figure out what *Noah's* Ark was doing in the story about Eli and Samuel.

15. Alter, *The Art*, pp. 114-130, especially pp. 123-124.

Chapter 2

Filling Our People's Heads With People[1]

The Development Of Character
In Sermons That Retell Biblical Stories

Another way to add things to a biblical story in order to preach by retelling it is to present more of a psychological portrait of a biblical character than the scripture usually gives us. Anita Diamant's recent best-selling novel, *The Red Tent*, aptly demonstrates the power of retelling biblical stories in this way. People are hungry for these kinds of stories. How do you as a preacher retell a biblical story emphasizing psychological aspects of its character(s)? Do you have to be a famous author or a licensed psychologist? Can you twist or obscure or diminish the gospel by assuming the motivations and thoughts and feelings of ancient people are like our own? You can.

David Buttrick, in his classic text, *Homiletic*, disputes the wisdom of attempts to "listen in on the articulate consciousness of a particular biblical figure" on several grounds. Events accomplished by God, Buttrick writes, get "dissolved into inner states or attitudes." Dramatic monologues, he objects, "almost always end in Pietism ... so that the mystery of God-with-us may gradually be edged out of the narrative and replaced by psychologies of faith."[2]

According to Bruce Malina and Richard Rohrbaugh in their *Social Science Commentary on the Synoptic Gospels*, people in biblical times "neither knew nor cared about psychological development and were not introspective."[3] Malina and Rohrbaugh issue their own stern warning against emphasizing psychological aspects of characters: "Our comments about the feelings and emotional states of biblical characters are simply anachronistic projections of our sensibilities onto them."[4] Thomas Boomershine, in his book, *Story Journey*, echoes these warnings: "[A] typical problem is reading our experience back into the story in ways that are incongruent with the biblical story. Appropriate connections grow out of experiencing the meaning of the story in its original historical context. To be authentic, the connection must ... relate to the meaning and life context of both."[5] At least Boomershine acknowledges that it *is* possible to make psychological connections with characters in biblical stories with some integrity, because for Boomershine, making such connections is an essential part of retelling biblical stories.

Still, it can be tempting to use a biblical text for the purpose of illustrating a particular "modern" psychological agenda. Yet, doing so can disengage listeners/viewers from the story. The incongruity of hearing a first-century biblical character talking about liberating "the child within" could lead listeners/viewers to suspect that the preacher is using the story for his or her own purposes rather than letting the story speak on its own. The moment of awareness of this incongruity is a moment when a preacher's intent becomes transparent. After such a moment, the listener/viewer can experience the rest of the story/sermon as a mere illustration the preacher uses for his or her own agenda. The story no longer speaks its own truth but is simply being *used* to illustrate someone else's truth. We'll talk more about transparent intent in chapter 5.

Approaching a biblical text with the purpose of illustrating a particular psychological agenda can not only distract listeners/viewers, it can distort biblical stories. It *can be* a way of projecting twenty-first-century sensibilities onto first-century people. It *can* violate the text's understanding of people. "Modern" people *are* qualitatively different kinds of people. Twenty-first-century people of Western cultures are motivated far more by individual identity and desires than were people living in regions surrounding the Mediterranean in the first century.[6] Malina and Rohrbaugh teach us that the identity of first-century people in regions surrounding the Mediterranean people was formed and driven entirely in reference to their social context.[7] People didn't sit down and fill out personal assessment exercises to determine their course and choices in life. Their identities and choices were completely bound up with an effort to maintain (not to advance or to reverse) their family's position in their community. Because people thought of the world

42

in terms of "limited goods," first-century peasants in regions surrounding the Mediterranean believed those who were advancing
their family's economic status by accumulating more goods than
others had to have been taking those goods from others.[8] Those
who were thought to be taking goods from others could bring dishonor upon themselves and their families. The rich, in a peasant's
point of view, were always robbers. A man might want to be rich
and might have the skills to accomplish this, but among peasants,
a man would not normally desire to bring suspicion and dishonor
upon his family by doing so. A woman might be brilliant at trade,
but among peasants, a woman would not normally consider a business career, because women could bring dishonor to their fathers
or husbands were they to act so independently in public. Perspec-
tives about wealth, the role of women, and other issues varied between rural and urban areas. Still, total submission to concerns
about family honor held sway in the regions surrounding the Mediterranean in ways completely foreign to twenty-first century people
in Western cultures.

People Are People

People are people, however. Richard Jensen makes this point
in his book, *Thinking In Story*. Jensen argues that it *is* possible to
make a "correlation between the human world and the biblical
world" simply because "the world of the Bible is not some other
world! ... God's revelation in Jesus Christ is correlated precisely
with human needs. God's work in Christ is the answer to the problems of life as we experience it."[9] There must be some connection
"between the human world and the biblical world," Jensen claims,
otherwise Jesus and the gospel would be completely irrelevant.
God certainly couldn't have wanted that!

Furthermore, in limited ways, people today still *do* act based
upon an understanding of the social consequences of their action.
In regards to ethical decisions, many twenty-first-century people
do *not* weigh the social consequences of their actions at all: *I don't
care what my parents or the rest of my family or my neighbors or
my pastor thinks; I'm going to live with my boyfriend.* However, if
it were to be a matter of keeping a job, twenty-first-century people

do understand very well what it would mean to act based on an understanding of social consequences of their actions: *my particular corporate culture demands a particular form of behavior; I'll toe the line and behave properly, because it's a tough job market* or *I need to feed my family* or *I like the money.* The similarities between the psychology of first-century Mediterranean peasants are as important as the differences. Twenty-first-century people *do* have references for understanding the struggles of ancient people in the proper psychological perspective, *if* such a perspective is accurately re-presented. This is the proper exegetical burden of those who would preach by retelling biblical stories in such a way as to emphasize psychological aspects of biblical characters.

Connecting With The Story

Here Boomershine's concept of "connecting with the story" is instructive. In his book, *Story Journey*, Boomershine believes that "generally our tellings of biblical stories are disassociated from human experience," and so throughout his book, he offers suggestions about how to connect our experiences of life with biblical stories.[10] For example, in order to make emotional connections with Luke's story of the birth of Jesus, Boomershine recommends that we remember or learn or share stories about births, or stories about opportunities we have had to tell someone some good news, or stories about political and economic oppression. Boomershine emphasizes however, that "in the absence of historical study, the connections people make with the stories are sometimes inappropriate ... Appropriate connections grow out of experiencing the meaning of the story in its original historical context. To be authentic, the connection must mutually relate to the meaning and life context of both. The story journey requires, therefore, that we listen closely to these ancient tales."[11] Our emotional experiences elicited by biblical texts have to be examined in light of the "historical study"of the text and what Boomershine calls "norms of judgment."[12] Automatically connecting romantic feelings with biblical stories about marriage, for example, could be a drastic misunderstanding of the norms of judgment of a biblical text. Because it was a norm that practically all marriages between first-century people were arranged by families, feelings of romantic love were not necessarily present in those marriages.[13] At the same time, there *are* many twenty-first-century people who could associate the path to marriage with feelings of having been forced to marry because of social pressures. Yes, we can make psychological connections with marriage stories in the Bible. But exactly what kind of marriage is the text about? The text must be the final judge of any connections we make with it.

Exceptions To The Rule

There are also many exceptions in biblical stories to the sort "honor maintenance behavior" among first-century Mediterranean peasants. Lydia was a woman who was brilliant at trade and who apparently pursued this gift to the point of being able to establish and/or sustain a business in a lucrative luxury item trade (Acts 16:14-40). Even among Galilean peasants, there were members of families who found it necessary to survive by means not regarded as honorable by authorities of various religious groups. When people were not landowners, sometimes they became shepherds — not generally regarded as an honorable profession.[14] When people were ineligible to share enough of the family inheritance to make a living, sometimes they became tanners or tax collectors — also not generally regarded as honorable professions.[15] When they were stricken with diseases like "leprosy," sometimes they became beggars.[16] When they engaged in sinful or shameful behavior like adultery, sometimes they became prostitutes.

Most importantly, Jesus himself *encouraged* people to act in ways considered shameful from the point of view of a first-century Galilean peasants and Jewish religious authorities.[17] If twenty-first-century listeners/viewers become aware of the powerful grip of the influence of "honor maintenance" on biblical people's identity because a sermon has fleshed that out by "psychologizing," how mysterious it begins to seem when people break with this social system to follow Jesus! That people followed Jesus at all *is* a mystery, but one discovered only when one "psychologizes" informed by social science — social science specifically aimed at understanding ancient people, not modern ones.

45

The sermon that follows this chapter attempts to do just that. It's a sermon in which I have tried to emphasize the psychological aspects of the character of Peter as presented in the Gospel of Mark and as understood by those who study the psycho-social make-up of first-century Mediterranean people. It's one of those dramatic monologue sermons that Buttrick discourages us from preaching. In it, I attempt to "articulate the consciousness" of Peter after having heard the first prediction of Jesus' suffering and death and after having just been called "Satan." In Mark, Jesus implies that Peter is one who "wants to gain the whole world."[18] Peter's attitude is clearly an exception to the whole "honor maintenance" way of life. Understanding Peter in the psychological framework of his context, we see a less traditional understanding of why Peter was so quick to abandon his family's fishing business and follow Jesus. That Peter follows Jesus wasn't necessarily a miraculous conversion as many Christians have traditionally viewed it. Instead, Mark's Jesus understands Peter to be a fellow who wants to gain the whole world and who sees Jesus as way to do so. That Peter is a man who wants to gain the whole world is also why Peter is so aghast when Jesus first explains that he will be crucified. Peter wants to gain the whole world; he doesn't want to be associated with a common criminal, but with a conquering hero. Gary, a member of my preaching group, vividly restates this understanding of Peter's character as he heard it in my sermon: "Peter thought Jesus was quite a power figure ... [Peter thought] instead of taking it on the nose all the time, why [didn't Jesus] do something to jack these people up? We're right, [Peter thought], and by golly, show 'em!"

The "psychologizing" in which I engage in the following sermon helped Gary see Peter as Mark portrays him. Just because Mark doesn't use dramatic monologues to convey who he believed Peter was, doesn't mean we can't — as long as what we say about Peter's consciousness is grounded in the text, not in our interest in using Peter's story to illustrate our own pet psychological theory.

Despite the psychologizing that goes on in the dramatic monologue of my sermon on Peter, the mystery of God-with-us is *not* explained away as Buttrick had feared it would be. When Peter finds out that he's not in for the big rewards he had been hoping for, why *does* he stick with Jesus? This is exactly the question that's on Gary's mind. "You *do* have to wonder why Christianity endured so long or grew in the first place, because you would think that what Christ was preaching wouldn't have flew at all ... Why didn't the [disciples] quit? So God's way must work ... otherwise it wouldn't have lasted this long. If [Christ] would have done the typical human thing, it probably wouldn't have lasted." Why Christianity lasted *is* a mystery. Why Peter stuck with it despite the fact that his human need to "gain the whole world" was thwarted *is* a mystery. Because I "psychologized," the listener/viewer was able to relate to the character Peter in a slightly different way and then come to wonder about the mystery of the survival of the Christian faith.

But there's more. In a "psychologized" representation of Peter, the listener/viewer can also realize in Peter's dubious and conflicted character how God works graciously with people who have the "wrong" motivations — forebearing them, forgiving them, gradually transforming them. Listeners/viewers can see and relate to Peter's struggle with selfishness and can wonder how he overcame those struggles to become a leader in the church. Listeners/viewers can be assured that as God had forgiving patience with one as conflicted as Peter was, God can have patience with them. Listeners/viewers can hope God can work with them in their own struggles to inspire them to become more faithful themselves. And that's good news, indeed!

Buttrick doesn't like "psychologizing." He and others say it's bad exegesis and that it *reduces* the mystery of God-with-us to psychologies of faith. But I have found that scripturally-based character study informed by social scientists like Malina and Rohrbaugh can create the true heart of a sermon that attempts to retell a biblical story *without* explaining away motivations of biblical characters. Furthermore, often an accurate and in-depth understanding of the psychological dimensions of the stories of biblical characters *deepens* the mystery of their motivation for following Jesus, because doing so was often so counter-cultural, so unusual, so unbelievable.

* * *

Peter Talks Back

A Sermon for Proper 19
(Revised Common Lectionary, Cycle B)
based on Isaiah 50:4-9a and Mark 8:27-38
preached at Our Savior's Lutheran Church,
Pulaski, Wisconsin

People in my world don't talk back to teachers like they do in your world. But I did. Me, Peter, son of a fisherman, I talked back to Jesus, the Son of the Ruler of the Universe. I rebuked Jesus just like he rebukes demons. I rebuked Jesus because he was talking crazy, because it's not just him that this Messiah thing is all about, it's about me! If Jesus gets himself rejected by the elders, the chief priests, and the scribes, if Jesus gets himself killed, what happens to me?

Jesus is how I make a living now. I left everything for Jesus. If I were to go back to my hometown, I'd have nothing. I'd be a big time shame there, dumping my family and civic obligations for Jesus as I did. I'd be worse than a joke to them; I'd be a criminal like one of those sex predators who get out of jail and the cops warn everybody where they live. Anyone who'd even to talk to me, much less buy fish from me, would shame themselves. People would yank out my beard and insult me and spit on me.

So I don't have anywhere to go except Jesus, and Jesus is talking about checking out. And that stinks.

Now let me make it clear. I don't have any regrets about losing everything. What did I lose? A really boring job. Mending fishing nets. Did you ever mend a fishing net? Did you ever sit around in the hot sun all day picking fish heads out of slimy rope? Or did you ever spend the whole day scraping the guts out of fish? You get this really profound sense of personal vocational fulfillment.

Jesus was my ticket out. Jesus was headed somewhere, I mean, with Jesus I've been all over Galilee, and now we're at the Roman villages around Caesarea Philippi, and I'm pretty sure we're headed for Jerusalem. Now, I've been to Jerusalem before. I get there once in a while, even though I know I'm supposed to be there every Passover. But you know, at Passover, there's like thousands of people there, and you're just a number, and it's crowded and noisy and stinks like burned up lamb guts. And you know, you've seen the priests cut one lamb's throat, you've seen them all. Even the prophets say that's not what it's all about.

But going to Jerusalem with Jesus, now, that's a different story. With Jesus, I'm going in one of those stretch limos with these huge crowds of Galileans following us who are gonna be full of pride about what we Galileans got. We got a guy who heals the sick! (Did you know Jesus healed my mother-in-law? Now that *is* a miracle!) We Galileans got a guy here who can put anybody back in their right mind! We got a guy here who can stop a tornado with a word! We got a guy here who can raise the dead! I mean, you just gotta have a little imagination about the possibilities here. We could say to Pilate or the chief priest or the emperor of Rome himself, we could say, "Hey, you want to live forever? We got Jesus. The Ultimate Insurance Policy. You treat us right, Jesus keeps you alive forever. You get your stupid army out of Israel, Jesus heals you when your friends try to poison your food." (That's what these Roman politicians do, you know. They kinda make the guys in Washington look like Big Bird and the Cookie Monster.) We could say to the Emperor, "Hey, if you invest in some infrastructure around here — some irrigation, some nice new schools, a new football stadium — then Jesus will keep you and your family happy and healthy forever. Work it out right, and that's what it could be. Now there's nothing satanic about that plan, is there? That's the beauty of it. Nobody gets hurt. We save our lives. We gain the whole world, and the whole world wins."

But Jesus doesn't like my ideas. When he got on his suffering and death stuff today, and I told him to get a grip, Jesus calls me Satan! Now that doesn't exactly do much for your self-esteem, does it?

But I don't see how him dying is going to accomplish anything. Why turn himself (and us) into a public humiliation? Why make us ashamed of him? We can't go around proclaiming the words of somebody who's dumb enough to get himself crucified! Man, this is just a dead end! When Jesus is outta here, he's outta here! Then what are we gonna do? What power do we have? And if they get Jesus, they can get us, too!

Though, now that I think about it, like I was saying, it really doesn't matter, does it? If Jesus is gone, they might as well string me up, too. I can't go back. All my eggs are in Jesus' basket. I'm dead meat without Jesus. So I'm gonna keep at him. Nobody's gonna tame Peter. Jesus can call me whatever he wants. I'm not gonna let him throw this away. Maybe there's something in the scriptures that can help me convince him to stick up for himself, to get him thinking about getting rid of his enemies.

(Peter picks up a Bible and opens it to a random page.)

Here. The prophet Zechariah. He's always good for stuff like that: "This shall be the plague with which the LORD will strike all the peoples that wage war against Jerusalem: their flesh shall rot while they are still on their feet; their eyes shall rot in their sockets, and their tongues shall rot in their mouths" (Zechariah 14:12).

(laughing) Awesome! I'll put a bookmark in his Bible right there. That'll teach him. Let's see what else I can find. I'll just open it up anywhere. Isaiah: "The Lord GOD has given me the tongue of a teacher, that I may know how to sustain the weary with a word" (Isaiah 50:4).

(sighing) That's Jesus. That's what he does. "Morning by morning the Lord GOD wakens — wakens his ear to listen, to listen as those who are taught. The Lord GOD has opened Jesus' ear, and he was not rebellious" (Isaiah 50:4-5 paraphrased).

Jesus *isn't* rebellious, is he? Not like Peter the fisherman. Jesus gives his back to those who strike him; Jesus gives his cheeks to those who pull out his beard; Jesus doesn't hide his face from insult and spitting. Because the Lord God helps him. Therefore, Jesus has not been disgraced. Therefore, he has set his face like flint. Therefore, he knows he won't be put to shame. Because the Lord God who vindicates him is near. Who's gonna contend with Jesus? Who are his adversaries? Because it's the Lord God who helps him (Isaiah 50:6-8 paraphrased).

That's Jesus. That'll teach me to read the scriptures. Jesus sustains the weary with a word. All the time. That's all he does. Are *you* weary? Are you sick? Are you the scum of the earth? Are you a couple sandwiches short of a picnic? Jesus'll sit you down, slice you a little bread, pour you a little wine, serve you up some dried fish, and then he'll tell you that you're loved and precious and forgiven by God.

And he drives the religious bigwigs nuts! He's gonna let them pull out his beard and insult him and spit on him and kill him. He thinks God's gonna vindicate him. Jesus thinks God's gonna make all his good words, all his good news, his *gospel* go on forever and ever. Jesus thinks we're going to be proud of the gospel and not ashamed of it. And, Jesus thinks we're going to go all around the world and say and do this gospel ourselves. He's not afraid of what others say about him or do to him. Jesus thinks God is with him, no matter what.

And I suppose that's what I'm supposed to be doing, right? Pick up the cross and follow Jesus and not worry about it and be brave and not return nasty words with worse ones and not rebuke my teacher and not ignore the study of his word, but just give it all away for his sake and the sake of the gospel, just give it all away for the sake of those words that sustain the weary. That's what I'm supposed to do: follow Jesus, no matter how inconvenient it is for my schedule, no matter how hard it is to find the time, no matter how embarrassing it is to say, "Sorry guys, the gospel comes first." Just follow Jesus — no matter what.

I don't know. What am I gonna do?

Chapter Notes

1. The title idea is taken from Richard Jensen's *Thinking In Story* (Lima, Ohio: CSS Publishing Company, 1993), p. 55.

2. David Buttrick, *Homiletic* (Philadelphia: Fortress Press, 1987), pp. 333-334.

3. Bruce Malina and Richard Rohrbaugh, *Social Science Commentary on the Synoptic Gospels* (Minneapolis: Fortress Press, 1992), p. 231; Thomas Boomershine, *Story Journey: An Invitation to the Gospel as Storytelling* (Nashville: Abingdon Press, 1988), pp. 20-21.

4. Malina and Rohrbaugh, p. 231.

5. Boomershine, p. 21.

6. Malina and Rohrbaugh, pp. 309-311.

7. Malina and Rohrbaugh, pp. 112-113.

8. Malina and Rohrbaugh, pp. 48-49.

9. Jensen, p. 92. See also Thomas Troeger, *Imagining the Sermon* (Nashville: Abingdon Press, 1990), p. 91.

10. Boomershine, pp. 37-38.

11. Boomershine, p. 21.

12. Boomershine, pp. 20-21, 36, 49, 90; "norms of judgment," p. 75. See also Thomas Troeger, *Imagining the Sermon* (Nashville: Abingdon Press, 1990), pp. 53-66.

13. Malina and Rohrbaugh, pp. 28-30.

14. Malina and Rohrbaugh, p. 296.

15. Malina and Rohrbaugh, pp. 296, 72-74, 82-83.

16. Malina and Rohrbaugh, p. 315.

17. Malina and Rohrbaugh, pp. 78, 313, 334-336, 345.

18. Walter Bauer, *A Greek-English Lexicon of the New Testament*, transl. William F. Arndt, eds. F. Wilbur Gingrich and Frederick W. Danker (Chicago: University of Chicago Press, 1957), p. 429.

Chapter 3

Filling Our People's Hearts With People

The Rhetorical Impact Of Character-Based Story Sermons

Every time I've watched Disney's animated movie *Mulan*, a song the character Mulan sings brings tears to my eyes. As the film begins, the creators of the movie are quick to introduce us to Mulan: a young woman who doesn't fit the role her society has set before her. A character, who appears to be the town matchmaker, conducts a test of the essential social skills for women in Mulan's society. Mulan fails the test. The matchmaker judges Mulan to be "a disgrace," to be completely unfit to be a wife. The matchmaker's words are cruel, but the test Mulan fails is rendered as light, satirical, musical comedy. I don't feel Mulan's pain when she returns home to mope around as her mother informs her father of Mulan's failure. Only when Mulan begins to sing does her predicament evoke an emotional response from me. As she sings, she's able to see a reflection of herself in a pond. She's still dressed in proper feminine costume and make-up, but as she sings, she sorrowfully wonders who she is if she's not who her culture wants her to be.

I think I was aware from the first time I saw the movie why these simple lyrics moved me so. Mulan's inability to be the person she feels she is reminds me of my interpretation of my own life's struggle. I'm not crying for a digitally animated, fictional character of eleventh-century China. I'm not shedding tears for Mulan, but for myself, for my own longing to be who *I* think I really am. During this song, I also feel for others dear to me in similar predicaments. I immediately think of gay and lesbian Christians I know who have been judged as a disgrace, who have sometimes broken their family's hearts by being who they are, who long to be pastors but cannot, because their denomination judges them to be unfit. The animated character, Mulan, and her predicament function as a catalyst through which my own painful story and the painful stories of others are awakened.

Let's Kick Some Hunny Buns![1]

Shortly after singing this song, Mulan seizes a role for herself she imagines she is more suited for: taking her aged father's place as a warrior in a war to defend her country. But neither her solution to her predicament nor the struggles it entails evoke the same emotional response as that initial song. I don't feel or think Mulan's solution is in any way helpful for me. Humor and suspense about the resolution of the action, not interest in the viability of Mulan's solution, keep me watching the rest of the film. Near the end of *Mulan*, I don't feel her triumph has been a lesson or a victory for me. "Let's kick some Hunny buns!" — the battle cry that signals the climax of the movie — is hardly an inspiring call to arms for me. At the end of the film, when Mulan's father proudly welcomes her home with a few simple words and actions, I respond emotionally again, vicariously enjoying her father's acceptance. It appears, therefore, that a character can sometimes evoke an emotional response for only part of a story.

Finally, that the words that evoke my first emotional response are sung may account for a large measure of their effectiveness. Simply reading the lyrics is not as compelling as hearing them sung and orchestrated; then they get to me every time. These rudimentary observations of my own experience of a story's character have much to do with a viewer/listener's experience of characters in sermons written as stories. More than plot, *characters* in sermons written as stories are the key to making a meaningful emotional connection with listeners/viewers. In his book, *Thinking In Story*, Richard Jensen articulates a profound theological justification for my point of view: "The people in stories come to live in our imagination. Hear how one student in one of Dr. Coles' classes described the reality of a person called Stecher from the trilogy of William Carlos Williams: '... to me, Stecher is — oh, now, part of me! What do I mean? I mean that he's someone; he's a guy I think of. I picture him and can hear him talking ... He's inside us ... Williams' words have become my images and sounds, part of me. You can't do that with theories. You can't do that with a system of ideas. You do it with a story, because in a story — oh, like it says in the Bible, the word becomes flesh.' ... Traditionally we have thought of filling people's heads with ideas. But we can just as well think of filling our peoples' heads with people!"[2]

It's Not About Plot

I have discovered other reasons to make character the highest priority specific to the practice of preaching by retelling biblical stories. One obvious challenge for those who preach by retelling biblical stories is that they must retell a story that listeners/viewers have just heard read as one of the lessons. Simply recapitulating the chronological features of a story would be boring. In the rhetorical context of preaching a sermon, plot does not have much potential to draw listeners/viewers into the sermon. People have just heard the plot. They know how it all ends.

Apart from the problem of the predictability of plot, my most plot-oriented parish project sermon drew the worst reviews. I retold the biblical story that surrounded Nehemiah 8:1-3, 5-6, 8-10 (Third Sunday After Epiphany, Revised Common Lectionary, Cycle C) with a meticulously scriptural focus on chronology. It's best to let the members of the preaching group speak for themselves:

Zandy: This was the first one of your sermons where I couldn't really stay on task through the whole first part, and I started floating away ... I was waiting for you to get dramatic ... You made [the story] more complicated. Could everyone else follow it?

Val: It didn't seem to have as much of a story to it; it just seemed like background, a history lesson, which is fine and interesting, but just sort of more factual, laying things out logically ... I still was a little disappointed that there wasn't more of a character for Nehemiah. In all your other sermons, you always had a character. [In this sermon] you didn't speak from a character persona.

I was genuinely surprised by the response of the preaching group. *Here at last I felt I had written a real story*, I was thinking, *because it has this truly grand plot right out of the scriptures!* After the preaching group's disappointing review, I was able to connect the dots between Val's observation that the sermon "didn't seem to have as much of a story to it" and her observation that I didn't present Nehemiah as a character. At least in terms of sermons that attempt to retell biblical stories, Val equates the term story with *character*, not plot. The sermon about Nehemiah had a plethora of plot, but no character and, for Val and most of the others in the preaching group, the sermon was not, therefore, much of a story.

Plots Consume Time

Plots are great for a ten-hour fantasy film trilogy that explains how two short guys with furry feet manage to save the world from evil. Sermons, in my denomination at least (the Evangelical Lutheran Church in America), are normally confined to a time slot of between eight and twenty minutes. Time, therefore, *is* a factor. A series of *events* takes a great deal of time to tell. Each event has characters, settings, and actions to describe. This consumes time. For the purposes of preaching by retelling a biblical story, if the term story is conceived of as a story of *character* and not as a series of events, events are recounted with the sole purpose of painting a vivid portrait of the character.

In one Reformation Day sermon, for example, I spent five minutes introducing the listener/viewer to a character by describing the first thirty or so years of her life. It was sort of a story, but not one made up of a series of distinct episodes. It was a summary of events: the character grew up poor, watched over her little brothers, and tried to get them to stay in school so they could get out of poverty. The story of how she escaped poverty herself took one sentence. Then I spent the final *ten minutes* on the *one* event of the sermon. By the standards of *Star Wars*, one event does not a story make; *The Phantom Menace* concluded with *three* events simultaneously playing out at one time! I'd like to see you try that in the pulpit! For the purposes of a sermon, *character* makes the story. The structure of time in retelling a biblical story need not, therefore, be evenly chronological or episodic. Half of the life of a character can zip by in five minutes, four to six years can zip by in one sentence twenty-seconds long, but one three-minute event can take ten minutes to tell, all because the point of a sermon told as a story is not an accurate sense of chronology but an intimate acquaintance with a character.

In the case of my Reformation Day sermon, after the listeners/viewers had a chance to get to know its main character and admire her, they could *feel* more deeply her struggle in the story's one *event*. This event forces her to choose between her hard-won convictions and the gospel. This gospel choice goes against her grain and against the grain of most listeners/viewers as well. When she finally does choose the gospel, this dubious choice is potentially validated by the listeners/viewers, because a character they have come to admire has made it. Once again, delving deeply into character can *intensify* the mystery of motivation, especially of motivations that go against the grain. How in the world did she make the compassionate, gospel choice she made? The listener/viewer is left thinking and feeling good about the possibility that it was *God* who made it happen. (This sermon follows ch. 6.)

Creating Characters Creates Problems

Creating characters, the heart of a sermon that retells or dramatizes biblical stories, creates some hermeneutical problems, particularly if one follows literary advice on the subject. Take the advice of my great friend, Winnie-the-Pooh, who says "It is the best way to write poetry, letting things come."[3] Anne Lamott, in her book, *Bird by Bird*, quotes Frederick Buechner who agrees with Winnie-the-Pooh about the poetic process of creating characters: "You avoid forcing your characters to march too steadily to the drumbeat of your artistic purpose. You leave some measure of real freedom for your characters to be themselves."[4] Lamott weighs in on the topic herself: "Fix ... on who your people are and how they feel toward one another, what they say, how they smell, whom they fear. Let your human beings follow the music they hear, and let it take them where it will"[5] and "... in lieu of plot, you may find ... you have ... a temporary destination ... you envision as a climax. So you write toward this scene, but when you get there ... you see that because of all you've learned about your characters along the way, it no longer works ... so it does not make the final cut."[6] When that happens, as it had in her second novel, Lamott gets "very quiet" and waits "for the characters to come to [her] with their lines and intentions."[7] Other writers make similar comments: "[Characters] take on a life of their own I kind of have to follow them."[8]

This is all well and good for novelists, poets, and Winnie-the-Pooh, but preachers have a purpose the drumbeat to which their work *must* march steadily. That purpose is sticking to a truth in a text. In *Bird by Bird* and other reflections about creative writing, one often reads that characters must be allowed the freedom to become themselves.[9] How can this work when a preacher's characters are given to him or her in a text that people are often fearful of changing in any way because of its sacred, revelatory character? What room is there left for real characters to be born and to exercise their free will to become who they are called to be? For me, it is once again, the intent of the text that must act both as guide and final judge of the characters who "happen." An important practice for those who preach by retelling stories is to compare their new story to the biblical story. Do the new elements in the story explicitly contradict what the listener/viewer will have just heard as the lesson or the gospel? Such explicit contradictions *will* be noticed and will *distract* listeners/viewers from connecting with the new story. They need to be removed.

Scripture Or History?

The sermon that follows is based on a pericope that Judas is explicitly characterized as a thief (John 12:1-8). As I prepared to create the character of Judas for this sermon, I asked myself the following question: as social scientists understand first-century Galilean society, what kind of person would have joined the Jesus movement *and* would have been or would have been inclined to become a thief? I did not ask this question with the intent of discovering who the historical Judas was but with the intent of discovering what kind of person the author of John's Gospel thought Judas was. This is an important distinction to make for two reasons. One: it gets people in the habit of thinking that there are as many valid interpretations of Judas as there are distinctive biblical stories about him. Instead of responding to the scriptures with a

58

quarrelsome anxiety for the "exactitude of certainty" that is not found in the scriptures, we can help people learn to celebrate what Kevin Bradt calls the "inexhaustibility of truthfulness" of a "narrative epistemology."[10]

Two: making the distinction keeps us focused on the particular story we're trying to retell. You're retelling *John's* story of Judas or *Luke's* story of Peter. Then, when listeners/viewers have questions about your retelling of a biblical story, you have a clear understanding about where each of the details of your story came from. You will be able to show them, detail by detail, that you are not being arbitrary, but faithful, and faithful not to "history" but to the scriptures! These kinds of conversations have been great teachable moments for me. Not being clear about this distinction can lead to misunderstandings and false expectations. For example, some of the publicity preceding the film, *The Passion of the Christ*, raised viewers' expectations about the historicity of the film. Maybe those who made negative comments about Mel Gibson's sympathetic characterization of Pilate did so because they were expecting a *historical* Pilate. The *historical* Pilate was a cruel man who would have never made deals with the religious authorities to try to save someone like Jesus. Gibson wasn't trying to present us with a historical Pilate; he was merely retelling Pilate's story following the relatively sympathetic renderings of Pilate in the four gospels. Those who critiqued Gibson's sympathetic portrayal of Pilate were judging a retelling of a biblical story using a standard of historicity inappropriate to the film. In their confusion, they missed an opportunity to critique the film on its most serious shortcoming: portraying *Pilate* as a "round" character but not the religious authorities.[11]

No Regrets For Judas?

I took my scripture-based question about the character of Judas in the Gospel of John and ferreted out of all the elements of his characterization. One of the most interesting results of this search was the fact that John does not report Judas' suicide.[12] Were Judas to have in some way expressed his regret for his betrayal, that would have been another dimension of his character to have taken into consideration. Such a complex character doesn't really fit into John's understanding of the world — an understanding which in pretty black and white ways pit "those loyal to Jesus" to "those in opposition."[13] I looked at the factors in the characterization of Judas in light of how a first-century author understood human psychology and began to wonder what sort of life would make a man both a disciple of Jesus, a thief, and an unrepentant betrayer. People heard the story of Judas as they've never heard it before, partly because they're used to hearing about the Judas in Matthew whose suicide adds a dimension of regret or despair to Judas' character — a dimension not present in John's story of Judas.

This Rat's Not Going To Last!

Should a preacher use Judas as the primary character in a sermon told as a story? Sensibly enough, Henry Mitchell objects: "Occasionally, Bible stories involved protagonists with whom we simply must not identify. Jesus did not intend for us to identify positively with the unjust steward ... rich man dives, or the elder brother of the prodigal son."[14] At best, for Mitchell, the purpose of "bad characters" is to "see ourselves in [them] ... only long enough to convict us and ... motivate us to become more like Jesus."[15] Mitchell also objects to an exclusive use of "bad characters," because for him, sermons must end with "celebration." "[In *bad* characters] where is the positive embodiment of the goal with which to launch celebration? ... Negative lessons then need to be paired with positive passages, so that there can be celebration relevant to the negative text's issue."[16]

For one of my project sermons, I *did* tell a story of "Rich Man Dives" so that listeners/viewers could see themselves in him. A member of my preaching group confessed that he *did* see himself in the "Rich Man Dives":

Dick: The whole thing is walking a line. My own perspective. I know how I am: how little can I do? How can I just fulfill the requirements and get by without having to jump in with both feet. The illustration of using the poor and the hungry so that he could on Sunday fulfill the requirements of the law by giving his own

60

servants the day off. He's walking the line! I could identify with the rich man. I saw his dilemma. As you're going through the thing, part of me's going, *this rat's not going to last* and part of me's going, *well, but you know, he is doing what the law says. Where's the wrong?*

But I did *not* drop "Rich Man Dives" for a more positive role model as Mitchell urges us to do. I let the rich man play out his self-righteous trajectory even to the point of insulting Jesus when Jesus comes down to the place of the dead to offer him forgiveness:

"The rich man is quite sure that this is a gang of thugs about to come to beat him, when he recognizes the man as the guest teacher in the synagogue, who had indeed, suffered under Pontius Pilate, was crucified, died, was buried, and had descended into hell. The guest teacher, beaten and bedraggled and wretched as he is, reaches out to touch the rich man, who draws back. The guest teacher speaks: 'You are forgiven.'

" 'Forgiven!?' shouts the rich man. '*I* am forgiven? Forgiven for what? And who are *you* to forgive sins? You're nothing but a common criminal! Who forgives sins but God alone? And in my book right now, *God* is the one who needs forgiveness, not me, because I have followed God's law to a tee to earn my everlasting reward and then I get this?' "

Because many listeners/viewers may have identified with the rich man in the beginning of the sermon as Dick did, the shock of the bitter and hateful way that he treats Jesus at the end of the sermon could have driven listeners/viewers to reflect even more seriously on their own self-righteousness and how it eliminates the need for Jesus and his forgiveness. If we can feel for a moment how little we need Jesus, we can feel how much we really want to get rid of Jesus, and how much we are in cahoots with those who wanted him dead. Similarly, Thomas Boomershine, in his book, *Story Journey*, is not afraid to suggest we can convict ourselves of the crucifixion, because the gospel writers did not hesitate to do so, either:

61

"The storyteller [of the crucifixion story] asks the listeners to recognize *our* corporate involvement in Jesus' death ... The primal connections of our experience with this story are experiences of consciousness and confession of personal and corporate sinfulness ... an awareness of human captivity to the powers of sin and death ... the awareness of our personal responsibility for Jesus' suffering and death ... the sinfulness of human communities, such as the nation and the religion....The story invites us to meditate on our involvement in the forces that cause war, racial oppression, starvation, sexual abuse, and poverty."[17] Do we, in the context of the sermon, need to absolve people of wanting to kill Jesus, obviously the most heinous crime imaginable for a Christian? Because there are other gospel moments in the rest of a worship service, I think the sermon need not always be the place that such angst is resolved. Why not trust the Holy Spirit to meet the person later in the service so that the assurance of God's love and grace is something sought and discovered on one's own and not simply proclaimed by the pastor? Barbara Brown Taylor appears to concur in this memorable succession of passages from her book, *When God is Silent*: "If we really love [our listeners], we won't bring them back much to eat. If we did that, they might mistake us for the Food Giver...."[18] Taylor instead, urges us to use "courteous language" in the pulpit. Courteous language: "respects the autonomy of the hearer. It also respects his or her ability to make meaning without too much supervision."[19] Taylor is not worried about leaving listeners/viewers thinking, wrestling with the implications of a biblical story: "Fortunately, the Bible is full of such raw and powerful stories. Maybe we should preach more of them, and where they are obscure, troubling, or incomplete, perhaps we should leave them that way...."[20] Taylor summarizes the implications for preaching: "Whatever preachers serve on Sunday, it must not blunt the appetite for this food. If people go away from us full, then we have done them a disservice. What we serve is not supposed to satisfy. It is food for the journey...."[21] For Taylor, it's all about homiletical, epistemological humility: "our words are too fragile. God's silence is too deep...."[22] Taylor concludes: "Only an idol always answers."[23]

Although I agree with Mitchell's description of the importance of giving listeners/viewers characters that are "positive role models" to emulate,[24] I don't think it's *always* necessary.[25] Boomershine is eager for listeners/viewers to experience complicity in the cross. Taylor is eager for listeners/viewers to experience the troubling silence of God. Richard Jensen recommends sermons that are "open-ended."[26] There's a clear diversity of opinion on the matter. Maybe it's a matter of pastoral discernment when to lift up "the good guys" and when to confront listeners/viewers with the ways that they're in league with "the bad guys." Certainly what the old cartoon character Pogo says is always true: "We have met the enemy ... and he is us."[27]

Making Bad Guys Look Good?

There are, I think, some good reasons to make "the bad guys" in biblical stories as attractive as possible. First of all, we shouldn't be in the business of demonizing biblical sinners. We don't want listeners/viewers to dismiss their own sinfulness by saying to themselves, *I could never be as bad as those people in the Bible!* If there are ways that people are still like the worst of biblical characters, it's important for us to exploit it. It's also important for us to transport people back into the biblical story so they can experience the gracious ways God usually deals with even the worst of sinners.

Secondly, what if a biblical character's sinfulness is painfully similar to the sinfulness of one of your listeners/viewers? If you ridicule or hate your "bad guys" in your sermon, your listeners hear that ridicule or hatred directed at them. You will have stopped telling a story and begun a holier-than-thou harangue. Your story will have become *transparent* to your angry agenda; the sermon will become more about you than about the gospel. (Yes, we'll get to transparent intent in ch. 5.)

Enough said about creating and connecting with characters. Please meet Judas again for the first time.

* * *

In The Garden

A Sermon for the Fifth Sunday In Lent
(Revised Common Lectionary, Cycle C)
based on John 12:1-8 and Philippians 3:4b-14
preached at Our Savior's Lutheran Church
Pulaski, Wisconsin

The disciples are allowed to enter Mary's garden through a stone arch barred with an iron gate. They pass into a fragrant, humid shade beneath palms, beneath trees bearing figs, pomegranates, and lemons, beneath trees blooming with orange, yellow, or purple tropical flowers. The sound of the dribbling water of a fountain, the cool scent of water evaporating on the fountain stone, the intoxicating fragrance of the flowers are all concentrated, hoarded inside high stone walls. It's another world; it's the world of wealth casting a spell on the disciples, causing them to forget the stench of the street: the animal excrement, the garbage dumped into it, the racket of creaking carts and braying donkeys and hawking salesmen and dogs barking and starving beggars clanking sticks on empty tin cups.

Judas had played in a quiet garden like this under the watchful eye of a private tutor. In a garden like this, Judas learned Hebrew poetry; he tried to play the lyre; he listened to his tutor play the lyre as it was meant to be played: notes flowing like ripples forming where drops of water fall. Birds sang. Breezes stirred the leaves, caressed the orange and yellow and purple blossoms that released their fragrance until little Judas' little world was all lovely lyre and the beauty of blossoms.

When his father lost his business and his home and that garden, he had a little capital left to invest in a few donkeys and carts and a clay and wood house with no courtyard garden, no slaves, no tutor, no lyre, just dirt on the floor and donkeys braying and donkeys defecating to provide fuel for the fire for their daily bread.

In Mary's garden, tears stinging his eyes, Judas remembers that childhood garden. The rest of the disciples are laughing, playing, splashing water from the fountain on their hot faces, on each

64

other. Then they seat themselves on cool stone benches under the shady trees as slaves come out to wash their feet.

Judas' grief flows as hot, bitter tears. This world had once been his. In taking over his father's business at age fourteen, Judas had worked ferociously, whipping donkeys mercilessly to get them to move as quickly as he could to cram as many deliveries into a day as he could. His father had died. His mother lived on the main floor of the clay house and cooked for Judas whenever he'd stop by for a meal and few hours of sleep in the guest room upstairs.

Gradually, Judas transformed the upper room into a tiny treasure trove. He covered the clay floor with red, gold, and purple Persian carpets he'd pilfered. Judas hung red and purple flowing silks he stole to hide the dull, sloping, clay ceiling. He burned frankincense and myrrh in golden receptacles. Judas even got his hands on a lyre, but it was only once in a great while he'd find the time to steal away to his upper room to keep trying to play it.

Judas was only one fourteen-year-old boy. The trade took its toll. One too many cart wheels ran over his foot. One too many donkeys kicked him in the face. One broke his leg. The cost of letting it heal drained all his assets. Judas lost his father's wood and clay house, his upper room of rich treasures, and his mother. He became a beggar lying in the street, his leg healing twisted and shorter. He banged on an empty tin cup with a stick.

One day some men came by and threw Judas on a cart and took him to Jesus who fed him by the shore of the Sea of Galilee. Judas clumped along after them, impressed with Jesus' fearless exposure of rich religious authorities who ruthlessly bought and sold foreclosed property of failed entrepreneurs like his father, and who'd turn around on the Sabbath and buy a brick or two for the new temple to soothe their consciences. Judas loved to watch Jesus get their goat.

Being fierce and knowledgeable about the tricks of mercantile trading, Judas was soon much beloved for his help in procuring daily bread for the disciples on their limited funds. Next to Jesus himself, Judas was soon much beloved for indulging the disciples with special deals he'd work out here and there along the way. Sure he took a little from the purse upon occasion, but it was easy to rationalize that and all the little treats — what they were doing for humankind far outweighed a few perks he was able to appropriate for the disciples and himself.

Jesus didn't indulge in any of the special provisions Judas provided: fresh breads, fresh meats, fresh fruits, a good wine now and then. As the disciples laughed and played when Judas produced plenty, Jesus sat by the fire, looking at it, poking it with a stick, and looking at Judas once in a while out of the corner of his eye.

In Mary's garden, Judas wipes away the secret tears he'd been crying for the home he'd lost long ago. Judas begins to hope that this garden is a sign that they were finally getting somewhere. Wealthy people, wealthy women had provided timely support for them all along the way. But to Judas, this garden begins to feel like it has corporate headquarters potential. Judas begins to wonder about sly Jesus who'd just raised Mary's brother from the dead. *Yeah,* Judas begins thinking, *now that we're out of the country, now that we're getting close to the capital city, Jesus dishes out a miracle here, a healing there, raises the brother of a couple of rich ladies — all to build himself a loyal coalition to finance the gradual seizure of a portion of political power, to build an alliance between himself and the ultimate power, the power of Rome. That's just what Herod the Great did. Why not us?*

Judas suddenly thinks he knows why Jesus seemed to have been especially kind to Roman centurions, tax collectors, and the like. In Mary's garden, Judas is figuring it all out for the first time. Judas is smiling at these thoughts as Jesus passes by him. The real Jesus smells stale compared to the fragrant garden. To Judas, Jesus is suddenly a smoky, sweaty stench passing by. Judas looks up at Jesus, who is staring at Judas sternly, as if he knows exactly what's going on in Judas' mind.

Mary, the wealthy hostess, comes out with a flourish of silks to greet Jesus, to welcome all the disciples to her home. She ushers them all into her house. Then Mary falls to her knees before Jesus. She produces a *pound* of perfume from a golden box that had been hidden beneath the flowing red and purple silk that envelops her. Judas eyes pop right out of his head. The fragrance of the perfume overwhelms everyone; it fills the entire room; it gradually causes each of the disciples in turn to fall silent, to turn to look at grateful Mary, kneeling before Jesus, massaging one of his feet with the perfume. Suddenly, with a shocking lack of womanly modesty, she releases the knot of the cord that has bound her hair. Her hair flows down around her, flows down around Jesus' legs as she massages his feet. She wipes Jesus' feet clean of days of dust and dung and Judas' eyes narrow. Judas now wonders if Jesus is up to something completely different, something he'd never seen motivate Jesus before. It accounts for his indifference toward them, his constant criticism of them. Judas is now thinking that maybe this has all been about Jesus snagging some rich lady, and pretty soon they'd all be expendable and Jesus and Mary would be living happily ever after in Mary's garden. So Judas says it; the words just spew out of sudden, jealous, hateful anger; Judas just barely has time to shape and control his words into something that sounds quite reasonable, almost polite. "I thought, my Lord," Judas says, "we were a common purse group. I mean, that fancy perfume there; I know I could have got a year's wages for it, *twenty grand* or more, to give to the poor."

Mary stops anointing Jesus' foot. She turns her head, holds back her hair, and looks over at Judas. She doesn't give Judas a haughty rich woman's look. Her look is apprehensive, fearful. She's wondering whether or not she's overdoing her devotion to Jesus a bit. Maybe she shouldn't express her love for Jesus, her gratitude for Jesus, so ... so extravagantly. Maybe her worship should be a little more reserved, a little more *Lutheran. Maybe*, she's thinking, *maybe I should have given the cost of this nard away to the poor.*

Mary looks up at Jesus, ready to do whatever he commands.

The disciples stand as absolutely still and silent as stones at this quiet challenge from a brother they love and respect for his shrewd business sense, for tending to their creature comforts on the long, dirty road. They like their roast lamb and just-baked bread and a fine wine now and then. They like their just rewards for all their righteous deeds. They like to remember all their great deeds, just as Judas liked remembering his father's garden, just as Judas liked remembering his upper room of rich treasures. None of them had yet learned to regard such memories as rubbish so that they might truly desire *Jesus*, so that they might truly love and worship *Jesus* as Mary did, so that they might truly know Jesus and the power of his resurrection and a share in his sufferings. None of them had yet learned what Jesus is all about: "forgetting what lies behind and straining forward to make the power of the resurrection their own and being grateful, grateful to Jesus that Jesus had made them *his* own" (Philippians 3:10-13 paraphrased).

Jesus says to Judas, "Leave her alone. She bought it so that she might keep it for the day," and here Jesus pauses, "for the day of my burial."

"Burial?" says Peter. "You must mean the day of your anointing! The day of your coronation!"

"Burial," Jesus says.

Burial, Judas thinks to himself. *Why burial? This is where we're going? Nowhere? To the grave? After all I've done for him?* Judas looks down at his own filthy feet, shaking his head.

Mary looks into Jesus' eyes for one awkward moment; then finishes anointing his feet, places the remainder of the nard in the golden box, rises, and addresses Jesus and the disciples: "We're glad you've come. How could we forget what you've done for us? Come in, all of you. Perhaps our bread and wine will help chase away all your dreary thoughts."

"Or perhaps," Jesus says, "The bread and wine will be for the remembrance of me."

Amen.

Chapter Notes

1. *Mulan*, produced by Pam Coates, directed by Barry Cook and Tony Bancroft, 88 min., Walt Disney Pictures, 1998, videocassette.

2. Richard Jensen, *Thinking In Story* (Lima, Ohio: CSS Publishing Company, 1993), p. 63.

3. A. A. Milne, *The Complete Tales of Winnie-the-Pooh* (New York: Dutton's Children's Books, 1994), p. 197.

4. Frederick Buechner in *Spiritual Quest: The Art and Craft of Religious Writing*, ed. William Zinsser (Boston: Houghton Mifflin, 1988) quoted in Anne Lamott, *Bird by Bird* (New York: Doubleday, 1995), p. 53.

5. Lamott, pp. 61-62.

6. Lamott, pp. 85-86.

7. Lamott, p. 86.

8. Bobbie Ann Mason, "Crafting Extraordinary Stories about Ordinary People" in *1997 Novel and Short Story Writers' Market*, ed. Barbara Kuroff (Cincinnati: Writers' Digest Books, 1997), p. 70.

9. Eugene Lowry in *The Sermon, Dancing at the Edge of Mystery*, describes a similar creative process at work in the development of "narrative" sermons, sermons that are not stories, but which are "sequenced" like one. Lowry uses H. Grady Davis' image of a sermon being like a tree to ground his idea that the sermon plot must have at its genesis a "generative idea": "During our preparation for Sunday, it sometimes happens that we get pushed out of the driver's seat of our own work and get taken for a ride ... surely it has something to do with H. Grady Davis' insistence that a sermonic idea has an expanding force ... and we get swept along." Eugene L. Lowry, *The Sermon, Dancing at the Edge of Mystery*, (Nashville: Abingdon Press, 1997), p. 54.

10. Kevin M. Bradt, S.J., *Story as a Way of Knowing* (Kansas City, Missouri: Sheed and Ward, 1997), pp. 179, 200.

11. It *is* disturbing that the character of the religious authorities was rendered so simplistically and unsympathetically. Gibson shows us no struggle to make the decision to seek the death penalty for Jesus — not even one based on self-interest which appeared to me to be what most of Pilate's struggle was about. Gibson needed only to use a few flashbacks to generate a sense of the profound conflict *Jesus* instigated among the faithful

people of Israel: one of Jesus' meals with tax collectors, prostitutes, and sinners or one of Jesus' trashing the temple would have sufficed to help viewers see things from the religious authorities' point of view.

12. Matthew is the only gospel writer who recounts Judas' suicide. Luke in Acts reports an entirely different story of Judas' demise. For a helpful summary of these stories, see M. Eugene Boring, "The Gospel of Matthew: Introduction, Commentary, and Reflections," *The New Interpreter's Bible*, Vol. VIII (Nashville: Abingdon Press, 1995), pp. 482-484.

13. Bruce Malina and Richard Rohrbaugh, *Social Science Commentary on the Gospel of John* (Minneapolis: Fortress Press, 1998), p. 31.

14. Henry Mitchell, *Celebration and Experience in Preaching* (Nashville: Abingdon Press, 1990), p. 47.

15. Mitchell, p. 47.

16. Mitchell, p. 47.

17. Thomas Boomershine, *Story Journey: An Invitation to the Gospel as Storytelling* (Nashville: Abingdon Press, 1988), pp. 170-171.

18. Barbara Brown Taylor, *When God is Silent* (Cambridge, Massachusetts: Cowley Publications, 1998), p. 110.

19. Taylor, p. 111. See also Childers, pp. 37-39; Jensen, *Telling the Story* (Minneapolis: Fortress Press, 1980), pp. 138-144; Jensen, *Thinking*, p. 115.

20. Taylor, pp. 115-116.

21. Taylor, p. 120.

22. Taylor, p. 121.

23. Taylor, p. 118.

24. Mitchell, pp. 101-103.

25. Mitchell, p. 47.

26. Jensen, p. 115. See also Boomershine, p. 52. Bradt, in *Story as a Way of Knowing*, reports Brueggemann's understanding of the epistemological orientation of the Old Testament: pp. 160-161, 200.

27. Walt Kelly, untitled cartoon for Earth Day 1971.

Chapter 4

My Mind Kept
Racing Back To The Bible

Hermeneutical Concerns
With Creative Ways Of Retelling Biblical Stories

When you're adding dialogue, characters, or events *not* in the biblical text, there's always a chance that your listeners/viewers with more literalist views of the Bible will find this an objectionable and dangerous distortion of the scriptures. Once a woman wrote to admonish me about one of my sermons, because she heard me say the star the Magi followed was a meteorite. (I actually said the narrator of the story may have been referring to a comet.[1]) Her admonishment was grounded in her understanding of the warning in the book of Revelation not to add to or subtract anything from John's prophecy: "I warn everyone who hears the words of the prophecy of this book: if anyone adds to them, God will add to that person the plagues described in this book; if anyone takes away from the words of the book of this prophecy, God will take away that person's share in the tree of life and in the holy city, which are described in this book" (Revelation 21:18-19). Thank goodness this warning only refers to the book of Revelation — although I had better watch out next time I preach on it! Her admonishment, interestingly enough, was also based on "the scientific fact" presented to her at a local planetarium that some sort of astronomical event *did* indeed occur on Jesus' birthday, an astronomical event that led the Magi to Bethlehem. How ready we are to acknowledge the truth of the claims of science! Despite the fact that I know of no biblical scholar rash enough to claim that he or she knows exactly when Jesus was born, the woman who admonished me assumes that *astronomers* know! If you insist on adding things to the scriptures, the more folks who have in your congregation who interpret the scriptures literally, the more chance there is that you may one day be admonished about this aspect of your preaching.

One Bad Apple *Does* Spoil The Whole Bunch

One bit of poetic license can damage a preacher's credibility permanently. For one of my project sermons, I retold a biblical story that I had meticulously based on the chronology presented by the book of Nehemiah. Despite my careful retelling of this biblical story, one of the group members reported that her mind was "constantly racing back to the Bible." She was, in other words, constantly wondering whether or not I was being faithful to the text. I later learned that her suspicion was generated by the dramatic monologue sermon on Peter accompanying chapter 2. After that sermon, she asked extremely pointed questions about my portrayal of Peter. Where she had always assumed that Peter had followed Jesus because God had miraculously changed Peter from a fisherman to a disciple, I articulated the interpretation that Peter followed Jesus, because Peter not so miraculously thought Jesus could help him pursue an upwardly mobile path. Those committed to literal or traditional interpretations may be troubled by anything that appears to disrupt their preconceived scriptural notions. Such concerns, in my experience, are not limited to one sermon, but spill over into sermons that are completely uncontroversial.

The crux of this problem with preaching by retelling biblical stories is a hermeneutical one. Do most of your listeners/viewers understand the Bible as a proof book full of proof texts to live by and full of accounts whose historicity is divinely guaranteed? Or do your listeners/viewers understand the Bible similarly to the way Walter Brueggemann understands it: "*We are not asking what happened, but what is said.* To inquire into the historicity of the text is a legitimate enterprise, but it does not ... belong to the work of Old Testament theology. In like manner, we bracket out all questions of ontology which ask about the 'really real.' It may well be ... that there is no historicity to Israel's faith claim ... we have ... few tools for recovering what happened and even fewer for recovering 'what is' ... those issues must be held in abeyance, pending the credibility and persuasiveness of Israel's testimony on which everything depends"[2] (emphasis mine). Here Brueggemann describes the Old Testament as a book of testimony of witnesses the truth of which is not proven, but that calls for our trust. When Brueggemann writes

72

about the *whole* Bible, he characterizes its entire text as a reliable witness to "prophetic construals of another world," an "evangelical world: an existence shaped by the news of the gospel."[3] As it is in the Bible, so Brueggemann thinks it should be in the pulpit: "The poetic speech of text *and of sermon* is a prophetic construal of a world *beyond* the one taken for granted[4] (emphasis mine). It is, Brueggemann argues, a kind of "fiction." He continues: "The notion of fiction, however, is not so precarious or easily dismissed as we might imagine. It is precisely the daring work of fiction to probe beyond settled truth and to walk the edge of alternatives not yet available to us."[5]

The Greatest Fish Story Ever Told

This is a marvelous framework for understanding a story like Jonah. Readers of Jonah could concern themselves with the question about whether or not humans can live in the stomach of a fish. Or one could read Jonah as a "prophetic construal of a world beyond the one taken for granted" by Jonah's hearers/readers, who apparently didn't think God was concerned about people of other nations. One could read Jonah as a fabrication of the truth that God *does* care about other nations and that the people of other nations and the fish in the seas and even the cows in Nineveh are considerably more obedient than the prophets of Israel! Among listeners/viewers with a hermeneutical orientation similar to Brueggemann, there may be less anxiety about adding things to the text in order to retell its stories. Those for whom the Bible is a historically accurate proof-book, however, will never be quite comfortable altering the text at all and therefore will never be quite comfortable with the practice of preaching by retelling biblical stories as I have described it here. If that's ninety percent of your congregation and you are committed to mastering this practice, it's probably time to start packing. It will do no good to goad such people for their "out-dated" biblical views by persistently preaching sermons that retell biblical stories.

To tell the truth, preaching a preponderance of sermons that retell biblical stories *is* a temptation for me, because for me, it's such an engaging and exciting way to preach. However, too much of *any* form of preaching gets predictable. Remember what the movie critics Siskel and Ebert used to say about being predictable! Preaching sermons as true stories from real-life incidents will be a refreshing alternative for those in the pew who fret about the poetic license involved in preaching by retelling biblical stories.

I have found that the vast majority of people in the congregations I have served (large and small, rural and urban) do *not* have such well-defined hermeneutical scruples of *any* kind that they're compelled to carp about my poetic licentiousness. Finally, demonstrating that you are "doing your job," that you are genuinely engaged in the pastoral tasks that confront you and the congregation, goes a long way in encouraging congregations to tolerate many sorts of homiletical experiments and inadequacies.[6] Practically every fan of one fiercely loved pastor I once knew readily admitted to me that their beloved pastor was one of the worst preachers they'd ever heard!

Were You There?

Another way of preaching by retelling or dramatizing a biblical story advocated by some prominent homileticians is retelling the biblical story as if the listeners/viewers were really there. Henry Mitchell describes this method in his book, *Celebration in Experience and Preaching*: "In my book, *Black Preaching*, I insisted that *all* narratives from the Bible ought to be told as if one had seen them. It makes no sense to expect the hearer to see the manger or the cross if the one who is preaching hasn't seen it...."[7] The purpose of this method is to "bring the hearer aboard, or into the experiential encounter" and is accomplished when "the preacher has already identified with the material and recounts it in an eyewitness mode." According to Mitchell, "often ... details were originally condensed out of the Bible account because of the familiarity with details that was assumed to prevail commonly among hearers of the oral tradition." These details can be found in "the biblical record" and "from study of commentaries and encyclopedias." Details must be "coupled with inspired imagination." Or to describe the process another way: "Our providing details is like putting the common substance called water back into the powdered milk. They are not the very same water or details that were removed, but they are so similar that the result is a very accurate portrayal."[8]

I certainly agree with the importance Mitchell places on knowing biblical characters as if "one grew up on the same block" with them. His description of "providing details" that were "condensed out" of biblical accounts, because they were "assumed to prevail commonly among hearers of the oral tradition" sounds a great deal like my project of fabricating the truth. My only concern with what Mitchell says is about retelling biblical stories in "an eyewitness mode." When I hear preachers tell biblical stories in "an eyewitness mode," I immediately feel as though the veracity of the message is contingent upon the believing the historicity of the story. The preacher appears to be telling me that Jesus *really is God* only because the miracles he did really did happen as they are being presented. The preacher is telling me the miracles are proof of the existence of God, of the divinity of Jesus. I don't believe that about the scriptures at all. If the historical Jesus did do miracles, it's as plausible to think of them being a function of his *humanness* as it is to imagine they are proof of his divinity. There have been countless healers or shamans in many, many cultures throughout the ages. In this Jesus is not unique at all. Believing that Jesus did miracles does not "save" us. Causing listeners/viewers to feel truth is dependent upon the historicity of biblical stories is as problematic for Christians who are comfortable with less literal approaches to the Bible as poetic license is for Christians who are loyal to literalist or traditional understandings of the Bible.

Between Scylla And Charybdis

In his book, *Plurality and Ambiguity*, David Tracy describes a phenomenon common to the context of listening to discourse he calls creating "victims of discourse." Discourse that explicitly assumes the historicity of scripture causes those with other assumptions to feel marginalized and even attacked.[9] Discourse that explicitly *denies* the historicity of scripture causes those with other assumptions to feel marginalized and even attacked. The point of the gospel is to gather and unite people, not to separate people on the basis of a particular hermeneutical understanding of scriptures. *The trick is, therefore, to retell a biblical story so that both points of view concerning the historicity of scriptures are possible.* If fabricating the truth is Scylla and making truth contingent on historicity is Charybdis, we need to bring our listeners/viewers safely through these straits without veering too closely to either danger. I am at present content to continue to sail close to the six-headed monster Scylla. Perhaps telling some good stories accompanied by some enchanting music will tame her. (It worked for Harry Potter and friends on a three-headed dog in *The Sorcerer's Stone!*) The truth is, not many people are particularly self-conscious about their hermeneutical principles. As part of the design of the Doctor of Ministry program I completed, I listened carefully to preaching groups, individuals, even whole congregations, and I rarely heard hermeneutical concerns about adding things to biblical stories, even from those who take the historicity of scriptures very seriously. Those who don't have literalist views of the historicity of scriptures, on the other hand, are more likely to be more conscious of their hermeneutical principles, because they have had to change them and define them from the more literal view of scriptures we all develop as children.[10] Making the truth contingent upon historicity is, therefore, more likely to be perceived. When it is perceived, it's my experience that it calls attention to itself; it's distracting; it's not persuasive at all. Making the truth contingent upon historicity is, therefore, the more problematic approach.

Finally, retelling biblical stories as if they really happened as they are written flies in the face of the diversity of versions of biblical stories. It assumes a standard of historicity for the Bible that was not known among biblical writers.[11]

"Blessed Are Those Who Have Not Seen And Yet Believe ..."

The second project sermon I did during my second year of my Doctor of Ministry studies was about Elijah's visit to the widow of Zarephath. This story concludes with a miracle: Elijah raises the widow's son from death (1 Kings 17:8-16). I include this sermon here as an example of trying to retell a biblical miracle story without creating "victims of discourse" among those holding either point of view concerning the historicity of scriptures. Rather than focusing the listeners/viewers' attention on the historicity of this miracle and making that miracle a prerequisite to believing a truth in the story, I didn't show Elijah raising the boy from the dead. Instead, the sermon ends with a knock on the widow's door and the widow hurrying toward the door, hoping, believing, and trusting that it *is* Elijah behind the door and hoping, believing, and trusting that Elijah's God might be able to continue to provide the possibility of life for her. Neither she nor the listeners/viewers have any *proof* that it's Elijah who is knocking at the door. Neither does she nor the listeners/viewers have any *proof* that Elijah's God would continue to help her. Like the widow, listeners/viewers are left with a picture of faith and hope: faith and hope is like running toward a God you can't see.

A member of my preaching group asked me why I didn't show the miracle of Elijah raising the widow's son, and why I ended the sermon with a knock on the door. In my answer I quoted the relatively well-known words from scripture below that were also part of the sermon: "In *hope* we were saved. Now hope that is seen is not hope. For who hopes for what is seen? But if we hope for what we do not see, we wait for it with patience" (Romans 8:24-25). The knocking on the door was the hope you can't see, and [the widow of Zarephath] ran toward it. We [the person playing the part of the widow and myself] thought that it was enough to indicate that she had embraced [God's] plan and that Elijah was back — although you don't see Elijah; you don't know if it's him — so it *is* a faith thing. We liked that sort of up-in-the-air faith thing ... well, is it Elijah or the Avon Lady? My comments elicited the following responses among the listeners/viewers:

Zandy: If you would have raised the son, then we wouldn't have thought so much.

Arlene: My granddaughter told me — she sat next to me — she says, "And you know what, [when the widow ended the sermon by exiting through the door] she left the door open a little bit so anyone could follow her."

That *is* one of the messages I wanted to impart: we are to *follow* the widow's example of faith; we are all *saved* by faith. Having the congregation eyewitness miracles may focus the attention of listeners/viewers on miracles as guarantor of the truth of the story. There are no such guarantors, only witnesses to trust, testimonies to believe, an invisible God in whom to hope.

What Is Truth?

One of the biggest hermeneutical problems with adding things to biblical stories in order to retell them, is that many listeners/viewers will come away from a sermon not really sure what exactly is scriptural and what isn't. Since most people don't know the scriptures very well, they won't be able to distinguish what about characters actually comes from the Bible and what are biblically based fabrications. The lie that Eli tells his sons, the life story of Judas — these are plot elements that people may remember about these characters. Do we really want listeners/viewers to come away from our sermons thinking that they've been told the true story about Judas? Do we need to print a qualifying statement in the bulletin? What would we say? Is this a real problem? It's a question I haven't yet explored with a preaching group, but I *do* have a story to tell about what goes on in the minds of some of our most sophisticated listeners/viewers.

Recently I preached a sermon on Psalm 139. I used the image of God as "knitting" humans together in our mother's wombs as the starting place for a conversation between God the knitter and his son Jesus. Not long after that sermon came our Ash Wednesday service during which members of our congregation received a cross of ashes on their foreheads to remind them they were made of dust. A six-year-old girl questioned her mother about this ritual. "Mom," she asked, "I thought we were *knit*." The conversation shows how much children really can and do hear in sermons. It also shows how they naturally understand such metaphors as literally true, because they are concrete operational thinkers. The little girl zeroed in on the contradiction that humans could not be knit and made of dust at the same time. Her mother tried to explain this concrete operational paradox to her daughter as best as she could, *but she also understood very well* that we are not *literally* knit together nor that we are *literally* made out of dust. Her mother understood that these metaphors were used and explored by biblical writers and by me to convey different truths about who we humans are. On a subconscious level, even adults who interpret the scriptures literally most of the time can see that the scriptures speak metaphorically or symbolically or poetically at times. Preaching sermons by creating conversations between God the knitter and his son Jesus *does* raise many interesting questions among listeners/viewers of all ages. I welcome every question as a teachable moment. These questions give people struggling with hermeneutical issues real motivation to attend one of the many adult education forums we offer to our congregation. In general, I think people are more curious than defensive; that their curiosity is aroused by this method of preaching can only recommend your attempting it.[12]

The fate of the widow's son is left open in the following sermon. The congregation, however, knows one thing for certain: the widow running to unseen hope for help is what the life of faith is all about.

* * *

The Widow Of Zarephath
A Sermon for Proper 27
(Revised Common Lectionary, Cycle B)
based on 1 Kings 17:8-16 and Mark 12:38-44
preached at Our Savior's Lutheran Church,
Pulaski, Wisconsin

(The Widow Zarephath is asleep on the left. She wears an old housecoat and ratty slippers and her hair is disheveled. Her son sleeps next to her. Somewhere off to one side there must be a door or an opening used as a door through which characters can enter and exit the sermon. The Voice of God, offstage, wakes her up.)

God: Widow of Zarephath!

(Widow starts, sits up, rubs eyes, and looks around.)

God: Widow of Zarephath!

Widow: *(irritated)* What? What do you want? Who are you?

God: I am Yahweh, God of Israel, God of Abraham, God of Isaac, God of Jacob.

Widow: Excuse me. My name is *not* Abraham or Isaac or Jacob. So you got the wrong number. I got my own god: the Almighty Buck. *(lifts up a huge dollar bill; shows the side with Washington on it first, then the other side)* See. It even says "In God We Trust" right on it.

God: You are the widow of Zarephath, are you not?

Widow: Yeah, one of them anyway. I got a *first* name, you know.

God: I'm sure you do. But they neglected to record it in the scriptures.

Widow: My name is Vanessa. Don't I look like a Vanessa? So, why am I having this conversation with Yahweh, the God of Israel and three dead guys, at two o'clock in the morning? A girl needs her beauty sleep, ya know.

God: I can see that. I'm calling you to put your trust in me. The famine in the land is my punishment upon King Ahab and Queen Jezebel of Israel ...

Widow: *(interrupts)* Excuse me! The people in *my* country Sidon are starving because the king and queen of *your* country, Israel, are a couple of crooks? I got a problem with that! Why are the people of Sidon starving because *your* people have a raunchy royal family?

God: I am Yahweh, Creator and Ruler of the Universe. I created all things very good. Sin wasn't *my* idea. The consequences of sin sometimes affect the guilty and the innocent alike.

Widow: Yeah, well that isn't fair. You think you could have done a better job creating and ruling the universe. My husband is dead at age 25. We innocent Sidonians are starving because your people got schmucks on the throne. Me and my son here are starving to death. Tell me that makes sense.

God: People always think they can do a better job at being God. Widow of Zarephath ...

Widow: *(interrupts)* Vanessa!

God: *(reluctantly)* Vanessa. My people are abandoning me for other gods. They ...

Widow: *(interrupts)* Jealous, eh? Well, I can see why. If my god would wake me up in the middle of the night to tell me what a lousy job he was doing, I'd throw him out the window.

God: My people are abandoning me for other gods. Their king and queen encourage it. I must reach my people before I lose them forever. I have found the best way to reach them is through other people. When people see a man or woman who has found the courage to give everything they have for my sake, people begin to believe I actually exist after all. People begin to place their trust in me. I am sending such a person to you. He is one of my prophets. His name is Elijah. The king and queen of Israel are seeking to kill him. I need you to help save Elijah, to sustain him during this famine, so he can return to my people with a strong body and a strong faith to turn my people's hearts back to me.

Widow: I see. So, let me get this straight. You want a poor starving widow who doesn't even worship you, who's not even one of your people, who has only a handful of meal in a jar left to eat in the whole house 'til who knows when, and you want *me* to give everything I have to feed Israel's "Most Wanted Felon" in *my* house so that he can go back to Israel *someday* and save *your* people! (*laughs*) I can just see this is gonna be my lucky day. So why me?

God: I have seen you at my house, Vanessa ...

Widow: Oh, yeah. I been there. I like gods. I check 'em all out. I shop around. You got a nice temple down there in Jerusalem. Nice sacrifices. Nice worship. Trumpets and lyres and timbrels. They write some great poetry about you, your people do. You must be some God for them. But there's just one small problem.

God: They won't let you in.

Widow: Right. Even if I was one of your people, I'd only get in as far as the court of the women. I wouldn't get in to see them sacrificing all those lambs and those bullocks and roast 'em. What's the big deal anyway? It's nothing I haven't seen in my own kitchen. I know. Those priests probably think we women are gonna steal their recipes.

God: It was not my intent that men rule over women. I created men and women to be equal partners. It was not my intent to exclude women or foreigners from the temple. Even King Solomon's temple dedication speech spoke of the temple as a place where all nations might come. But these intentions have not yet been realized. I must be patient. People are not puppets. I cannot force them to do as I command. People want to have things their way. People want to obey their thirst. People want to do their own thing.

Widow: Yeah, and the whole world's at each other's throats. Everybody wants things their way. You can see it all over the place. Liberals and conservatives fight each other in every government and in every religion; Catholics and Protestants are fighting in Ireland; Palestinians and Israelis are fighting in Israel. Everybody thinks they're better than everybody else; everybody thinks their temple is better than everybody else's. And guess what? Everybody's so busy fighting, we poor folks starve. The innocent suffering for the guilty, again. And so what are *you* gonna do about it?

God: Through Abraham, through his family, through my people, all the families of the earth will be blessed, will one day be one. You will help my family survive to keep my plan alive.

Widow: Yeah. Right. One heck of a plan. A starving foreign woman gives everything away to save your prophet's posterior. Get outta here!

(Elijah enters from the right and knocks on the door. Widow starts, looks at her alarm clock, slams it down on the table, and goes to the door.)

Widow: It's a little early for trick or treat. Whaddaya want?

Elijah: Bring me a little water in a vessel, so that I may drink. Bring me a morsel of bread in your hand.

Widow: (*aside*) Not even a "Good morning, how are ya?" Just comes in here and expects me to serve him like I was his slave. *(to Elijah)* You must be the prophet Elijah, right? Excuse me. But as the Lord your God lives, I have nothing baked; I only have one handful of meal in a jar, and a little oil in a jug; I was just gonna go out and gather a couple sticks, so I can make a little breakfast for me and my son, so we can eat it, and die. I don't have anything for you! Why don't you go out and get a job and work for it like the rest of us?[13]

Elijah: Do not be afraid; go and do as you have said; but first make me a little cake of meal and bring it to me, and afterward make something for yourself and your son. For thus says the Lord, the God of Israel: "The jar of meal will not be emptied and the jug of oil will not fail until the day that the Lord sends rain on the earth."

Widow: Oh. So that's the deal. If I give away everything for your God, if I trust in your God, he'll look after me so his plan gets accomplished. Okay. All right. I'll make you your cake. I'll give you everything I have. What do I got to lose? Then I'll go out and I'll get some sticks, and if I come back and that jar isn't full, you'll be outta here so fast it'll make your head spin.

(Widow leaves Elijah standing in the doorway, returns into house to mix the last of her flour and oil and roll it out as dough — there's a pitifully small amount — as she works she addresses Elijah.)

Widow: See? This is all I got. The whole nine yards. It's all yours! *(goes to Elijah and slaps a doughy ball in his hand)* Now you sit out here and wait 'til I get back. I don't want have my son waking up with some goofball guru sitting in the living room. He'll think his mother's flipped her lid. And remember what I said about that jar of meal!

(Widow exits right. Elijah enters the house, leaves a full jar of meal that has been concealed under his cloak; then he exits to the right as well. Widow then returns from the right with a pile of sticks. As she enters the house, first she sees the full jar of meal then she looks at her son, drops the sticks, rushes to him, puts her hand down on his forehead, seats herself disconsolately at his side, and continues her part.)

Widow: So this is how that God works. Gives me a full jar of meal for his lousy prophet, but then takes away my son because of my nasty mouth. I can take my own punishment. But my son. He didn't do anything. He didn't do anything to deserve hunger, starvation, death. There we go again. The innocent suffer for the guilty. Elijah can have his stupid jar of meal. I'm not eating it.

God: Vanessa.

Widow: Oh, look who shows up again. You know, your system stinks. I give away everything for your plan and then what happens? Do I get a nice reward for my trust? Do I get a nice reward for my good works? No, it looks like I get punished. Or worse, the innocent suffer for the guilty again. Somebody dies for the sins of others. We *all* starve to death because of some lousy government.

God: I am sorry, Vanessa. I'm not happy about the suffering of the innocent. I don't know your pain now, but one day I will.

Widow: Serves you right.

God: One day I will have a son, a beautiful son like yours, Vanessa.

Widow: *(aside)* I pity the gal who gets mixed up with this god.

God: My son will come to the temple. It will be a bigger and more beautiful temple even than Solomon's temple. My son will see, however, how my house will be used to build up the rich, how it will be filled with money changers from whom the poor must buy forgiveness at outlandish rates, how it will be an institution in which the rich invest to make their names look great, how it will continue to exclude women and the poor and those whose bodies or minds are not whole, how it will exclude those of other races and tongues. My son will speak out against this temple, against all such temples, against this way of life. My son will heal and forgive and welcome those who are cast out by the temple authorities. He will invite and bless all the families of the earth; he will work to unite them as one family, as *my* family. In my son, there will be no longer be conservatives or liberals, Protestants or Catholics, Israelis or Palestinians; there will no longer be poor or rich, there will be no longer male or female; for all will be one in Christ Jesus, my son, their Lord. But for his efforts, my son will be killed. My son, like your son, will die, a most cruel, undeserved death. I am so sorry, Vanessa. It will not be long and I too, will be torn with grief as you are now, torn with grief to see them beat my son, strip

85

him, crown him with thorns, pound nails through his wrists and ankles, and mock him. All because he gave everything for this my plan.

Widow: Been there. Well, I tell ya: I'll believe it when I see it.

God: You will believe. But now, Vanessa, now I have chosen *you* to be part of my plan. I must make you strong so Elijah will be strong so my family will be strong and survive until the day my son comes. The meal in your house will not run low. Your son, who has died an innocent victim of sin, your son shall be raised. Elijah will return soon to do so. By my power your family will be blessed and one by one, little by little, all the families of the earth will stop their quarreling and be blessed, and will become one, one in me, one in my son.

Widow: I'll believe it when I see it.

God: You will believe, Vanessa. But now your real challenge is just like mine. To believe even when you don't see it. Hope that is seen is not hope. For who hopes for what can already be seen? (Romans 8:24 paraphrased). Those who have hope look not at what can be seen, but at what cannot be seen. What can be seen is temporary, but what cannot be seen is eternal (2 Corinthians 4:18 paraphrased).

(Elijah knocks on the door. Widow starts and looks up toward the door with hope and amazement. Elijah knocks again, louder. Widow looks down at her son again, smiles, rises, and holds up her hand.)

Widow: Wait! Oh, God, I hope it is ... wait! Don't go away! I'll be right there!

(Widow exits through door)

Chapter Notes

1. M. Eugene Boring, "The Gospel of Matthew," in the *New International Bible*, Vol. VIII, Leander E. Keck, et al. eds. (Nashville: Abingdon Press, 1995), p. 350.

2. Walter Brueggemann, *Theology of the Old Testament: Testimony, Dispute, Advocacy* (Minneapolis: Fortress Press, 1998), p. 118; Kevin M. Bradt, S.J., *Story as a Way of Knowing* (Kansas City, Missouri: Sheed and Ward, 1997), pp. 160-161.

3. Walter Brueggemann, *Finally Comes the Poet: Daring Speech for Proclamation* (Minneapolis: Fortress Press, 1989), pp. 4 and 3.

4. Brueggemann, *Poet*, p. 4.

5. Brueggemann, *Poet*, p. 5.

6. Lucy Lind Hogan and Robert Reid, *Connecting with the Congregation: Rhetoric and the Art of Preaching* (Nashville: Abingdon Press, 1999), pp. 47-67.

7. Henry Mitchell, *Celebration and Experience in Preaching* (Nashville: Abingdon Press, 1990), p. 89.

8. Mitchell, p. 40.

9. David Tracy, *Plurality and Ambiguity* (Chicago: The University of Chicago Press, 1987), p. 79.

10. Robert C. Fuller, *Religion and the Life Cycle* (Philadelphia: Fortress Press, 1988), p. 32.

11. David Rhoads, *The Challenge of Diversity* (Minneapolis: Fortress Press, 1996), p. 3.

12. Richard Jensen, *Thinking In Story* (Lima, Ohio: CSS Publishing Company, 1993), p. 115. See also Thomas Boomershine, *Story Journey: An Invitation to the Gospel as Storytelling* (Nashville: Abingdon Press, 1988), p. 52 and Kevin M. Bradt, S.J., *Story as a Way of Knowing* (Kansas City, Missouri: Sheed and Ward, 1997), p. 200.

13. Thanks to Arlene from Our Savior's, Pulaski, Wisconsin, for this great line!

Chapter 5

I See What You Mean

Factors Affecting "The Willing Suspension Of Disbelief"

In the course of my Doctor of Ministry program, I experienced a method of preaching by retelling a biblical story attempted by a colleague, a method that did *not* work for me, at least in the example that he used to demonstrate it. In the example of his method, the preacher pretended that he was Lazarus, dead in the tomb, dreamily listening to Jesus' attempts outside the tomb to raise him. As a dead man, the preacher reflected on the human struggle against several kinds of "death" we experience in daily life: the struggle to survive in our dog-eat-dog world, the struggle to sustain relationships, and the struggle against disease, addiction, and despair. The preacher, as Lazarus, spoke about how difficult it is for us to hear Jesus offering to free us from these familiar human struggles. As Lazarus struggled to hear Jesus calling him, so we struggle to hear Jesus calling us. I knew all along that Jesus would finally get through to Lazarus. I knew all along that the message would be that "Jesus delivers us from sin and death." Predictably enough, at the end of the piece, Lazarus heard and obeyed Jesus and came out of the tomb. Sure enough, Jesus delivers us from sin and death! Certainly it's a true statement. Isn't the truth enough? Ironically, since the truth was so perfectly clear, all that remained for me to focus on during the sermon was how the preacher was pretending he was a dead guy in the first century who was thinking about all the problems people face in their daily lives in the twenty-first century who was also listening to Jesus try to get him to wake up. Instead of challenging me about the ways I'm not really alive but dead, I experienced the whole sermon as a clever rhetorical game. Yes, I came away with the moral of the story, a simple didactic statement: Jesus delivers us from sin and death. But for me, once again, the truth was *not* enough. I could not relate to a dead biblical character talking about the difficulties of life in the twenty-first century; I did not come to care about

Lazarus. I simply saw *through* his story. I saw the preacher *using* the story as an illustration, an allegory. The story became *transparent* to his intentions.

Transparent Intent And Willing Suspension Of Disbelief

Perhaps this sermon about Lazarus illustrates one of David Buttrick's legitimate concerns about sermons that are stories. In his book, *Homiletic*, Buttrick observes that "few of us are skillful enough to tell a story in such a way that *theological* meaning forms."[1] Stories in which theological meaning is formed *are* difficult to create. Over the last four years of trying to learn this craft, I have found myself constantly tempted to lose faith in the stories I've been telling and resort to inserting various old-fashioned didactic ways of telling the truth. In the sections that follow, you'll see examples of the many different ways that you, too, may be tempted to lose faith in the story.

When a story *is* well told, listeners/viewers "willingly suspend their disbelief" and begin believing that the world and the struggle of the story and its characters *is* the real world happening before their eyes, so much so that they come to love or hate or cry for or worry about its characters.[2] Willing suspension of disbelief happened for me in parts of the movie *Mulan*. If there are any signs in the story that the preacher is trying to *use* any element of the story for hammering home any kind of agenda, the listener/viewer no longer remains *in* the story, but can see *through* the story; the preacher's intent becomes transparent in an annoying way. The listener/viewer then becomes focused on the preacher and his or her clever plan to use the story and its characters, or the listener/viewer becomes focused on the preacher's agenda and whether the listener/viewer agrees with it or not. The listeners/viewers no longer focus on or respond to the characters in the story. Because listeners/viewers no longer feel for the characters in the story, they can no longer *feel* the gospel for them, and the story's ability to reach the heart and soul is impaired. And this, after all, is the reason for preaching as storytelling in the first place. So Richard Jensen reminds us: "Sinners ... don't want information about help ... Sinners want help! They want to hear a word that sets them free; that forgives their sins; that gives them resurrection life ... But, too often, our preaching just talks *about* the announcements Christ made. We talk about Christ's announcements as if they are in the past rather than proclaiming them as realities of the present moment of preaching."[3]

Monkeying With The Story Boards: Transparent Intent And Plot

One of the most obvious problems with preaching by retelling or dramatizing biblical stories has to do with plot. Most often, one preaches on one of the lessons just read to the congregation. If one of those lessons contains the story the preacher is about to tell, how can the story be told again without being a predictable recapitulation of the story? All along the listeners/viewers know how the story ends. How can such a story keep the listeners/viewers' interest? Those who remember Gene Siskel and Roger Ebert's lively discussions of films will recall how often one or both of them were dismayed when plots were predictable. When a plot is predictable, listeners/viewers are aware that they are pretty sure they know what the storyteller is going say next. When listeners/viewers experience this awareness, they can begin to feel detached from the story; they can begin to feel like they see through its plan; the storyteller's intent is then transparent. I experienced a particularly glaring example of this at the end of Disney's animated version of *Tarzan*. I remember feeling manipulated by the rapid alternation between two possible endings: Tarzan stays in Africa with his friends *or* Tarzan goes to England, gets married to Jane, and becomes an Episcopalian. I could just see the creators of the film monkeying with their storyboards in the Disney studios. Their intent was transparent: they were trying too hard to heighten suspense. It ruined the movie for me. My attention was focused on the intent of the storytellers. I no longer cared about the fate of the story's characters.

Because the heart of sermons which attempt to retell biblical stories is to generate an emotional connection to character and is not so much about creating an elaborate plot, concerns about manipulating plot are minimalized simply because there's not a lot of plot to plot.[4] Pretty often, plot *will* usually need to be added to the retelling of a biblical story simply because pericopes are so small in scale, but also because they do not reveal much about characters in the story (as David Buttrick rightly pointed out). But the purpose of plot in sermons that retell or dramatize biblical stories is *only* to create character. Whatever plot must be made up must, of course, be guided by how the character is presented in the scriptures.

Some story forms or genres appear to me to be particularly unsuitable for sermons, because their predictability can break the spell a story can weave. "The Christian Story" can be told in a very predictable manner: the sick get healed; sinners repent and are forgiven; the cross is followed by a resurrection. Listeners/ viewers can drearily figure out the ending of such plots long before the sermon is over. Such stories can appear to be contrived, fake, too good to be true. Certainly the movie *Titanic* had a problem with predictability (it perhaps even flaunted its predictability) and yet it was able to attract huge numbers to see it again and again. However, filmmakers can draw on many resources preachers generally cannot. It can be a challenge to make the Christian "myth" a true surprise.[5]

However, "the Christian Story" can also be *un*predictable; it *can* have a surprise ending; it *can* be a parable or parabolic as John Dominic Crossan and Herbert Anderson and Edward Foley define it.[6] Sometimes the good guys don't turn out to be who we think they should be; sometimes God or Jesus forgives and loves sinners we'd rather not see forgiven and loved. The Jesuses and Christs of the canonical New Testament use many genres to achieve what Crossan calls a "subversive" rhetorical effect to undermine the prevailing worldview to make way for the gospel. The beatitudes claim that the poor and meek are blessed (not the rich and famous); prophecies proclaim that the powerful will be cast down; parables lift up the acts of apostates as examples of God-pleasing behavior; narratives describe traitorous con men being changed into humble, grateful God-pleasers; teachings suggest those who insult others are no better than murderers; and so on. Such surprise endings are fine if a story is only a minute long or so, like Jesus' parables. But simply giving a story that's fifteen minutes long a surprise ending doesn't guarantee listeners/viewers will still be interested in the story at its end. Surprise endings can also feel contrived. Still, exploiting opportunities such "parabolic truth" offers might be a good way to design plots that keep listeners guessing all along.

Now Don't Make A Spectacle Of Yourself!
Transparent Intent And The Preacher As Performer
Another form of transparent intent has to do with the actual presentation of the story or drama. If the preacher as storyteller or actor calls attention to him or herself through his or her presentation, then the preacher has failed. I recall a classmate who vigorously, desperately presented his case that people ought to come to worship. The more vigorously and desperately he presented his case, the more I began to focus on him: the way his presentation was wearing out his voice, the way sweat was forming as little beads on his forehead, the way his shirt became soaked with sweat. This also happens when storytellers or actors "overact," thinking the point of the performance is to show off their skills rather than to *be* a character. These kinds of presentations become transparent in a way that the listeners/viewers see either a pathetic or impressive performance of a "Hollywood Wannabe" and do not hear the gospel. The point of preaching is to convey the gospel, not to be an outlet for a frustrated actor. In her book, *Performing the Word*, Jana Childers talks about "unselfish performers" who completely submit themselves to understanding the physiological aspects of oral performance and to understanding the text. This reverent dedication to performance is not about "strutting your stuff." For "unselfish performers," the "what" of performance completely eclipses the "who" of it.[7] The "what" in the case of a preacher is the gospel. Preachers who retell or dramatize biblical stories must be brutally honest about the practice and must always prayerfully keep the point of preaching in this manner before them and before those who work with them.

In her book, *Performing the Word: Preaching as Theatre*, Jana Childers also describes of the concept of "distance." For Childers, neither theater nor storytelling are occasions for "in your face" moralistic harangues. Such harangues are also invitations for listeners/viewers to suspend their disbelief and see through the story to the preacher.[8]

Transparent Intent And Dialogue

Discipline is also necessary when writing dialogue. Often one is tempted to use dialogue to "get the point across" so characters sound like they're preaching a sermon or delivering a theological lecture. Effective dialogue should seem real, should be composed of words and sentences real people use. Effective dialogue will not call attention to itself or its intent or the clever writing style of its composer. Henry Mitchell puts it perfectly: "The people hear the word as alien, and relate to the speaker in the same way."[9] Mitchell makes another excellent point I had not considered: "This insight is evident in the way some people relate to youth. No matter how old the speaker is, the use of the latest youth lingo will procure her or him a bond with the teenagers."[10] Still, the use of "the latest lingo" can be a precarious strategy. The "latest lingo" changes rapidly. Using last year's lingo is a signal that you know some lingo, but you aren't really keeping up with it, and that you're just *using* lingo to try to make a connection with youth. Kids will see through that. It's an interesting example of transparent intent. If you *do* use the latest lingo, it *is* as effective as Mitchell claims it is, but needs to be acquired from genuine and constant acquisition of it.

My Doctor of Ministry advisor Connie Kleingartner alerted me to the temptation to resort to theological discourse and jargon in a speech in one of my first project sermons. The following lines of dialogue in bold face are ones I have identified for editing. These lines of dialogue contain archaic, overly formal, polished or "melodramatic" language, overly complicated sentences, or rhyming words — constructions not generally characteristic of conversational speech patterns.[11]

... now, for the first time Peter mourned. Though festooned in rich robes, King Peter was poor in spirit and he mourned and hungered for the just, balanced, righteous way things had been.

The archbishop gently said to Peter, "You were so caught up by what you thought you could be, you forgot who you were: a boy who had just lost his father. You tried to **escape your grief and fears** with ambitious building **schemes that consumed you and your people** and your land. You **once** said you were blessed because you built your kingdom. You are **blessed instead**, now that you mourn over it. **For what but your mourning makes you merciful? What but your mourning makes you mindful of the plight of those down there? And what but your mourning makes you hunger for righteousness?** And **what but your mourning purifies your heart, washing all the bitter salt out of it in tears? What but your mourning, King Peter, makes you long for peace?"**

"Peace," sighed King Peter gesturing to the angry advisors arguing at the Redwood Table, "and how **shall** I make peace? I'm an orphan. **I have no father** to teach me **the way of peace** that somehow he **established in this land and that I have now destroyed."**

"Blessed," said the archbishop with a smile, "are those who have **resolved** to make peace, for they will be called children of God. You *have* a father, Peter, a father in heaven, **a father** who mourned the loss of his own son, but whose own son now lives again, **a father** and son who now **shall** never die, **a father** whose kingdom **is for** the poor in spirit, is for those whose spirits are **absolutely impoverished** and can do nothing but beg."

"That is indeed, who I have become, a king of beggars." Peter turned again to look again upon the ravaged hillsides, the dead rock mountains like a prison wall, the grim, armed guards in the streets, the desperate faces of beggars, of exhausted men, and of well-dressed women selling their bodies for gold.

The archbishop continued, "Peter, come with me to the Church on the Hill. **You've not been** there for a **very** long time. It's like your father's inn **of old**. Tell your story **there in prayer** before the free and magical meal in which you become one with your father in heaven. It's **the communion** of the saints, **the communion** of the blessed; **the communion** of those who have no kingdom on earth, **for the legacy of such kingdoms is at best ambiguous.**

Instead of striving for such kingdoms, the communion of saints has instead been *given* kingdom, an everlasting feast in heaven the **foretaste of which, dear Peter**, child of God, is in the meal in the Church on the Hill."

Although I still like the general point of the conversation, my advisor suggested that the complex, formal nature of the speeches might call attention to themselves and not to the gospel they are meant to convey.

Transparent Intent And Pastoral Trust

Finally, sometimes one listener/viewer will "willingly suspend their disbelief" while another will not, depending upon one's relationship with the preacher. A bond of trust must exist between listener/viewer and preacher for stories to work. If a preacher shows little pastoral interest in members of a congregation nor seems to have a stake in its overall fate, the pastor's storytelling abilities can quickly be perceived as trying to show-off. It's risky to tell the truth by making up ways to retell biblical stories; pastors who are respected for their work and dedication will more likely have more freedom for innovation.[12]

The sermon that follows is based on a story that the congregation will have just heard: the story of the rich man and Lazarus. For this sermon, I created a character who incarnates some theological concepts my congregation of primarily middle- to upper-middle-class people often find attractive: God blesses the obedient with success; the misery of poverty is God's just punishment for the depravity and laziness of the poor. The rich man takes this worldview beyond the framework of the biblical story to the biblical/creedal story of Jesus who descends into hell to make "a proclamation to the spirits in prison" (1 Peter 3:18-20). The attractiveness of the rich man caused many in the preaching group to pity him and/or identify with him ... at least until they realized that to do so was to set themselves against Jesus.

*   *   *

The Rich Man And Lazarus
Go To The Other Side
A Sermon for Proper 21
(Revised Common Lectionary, Cycle C)
based on Amos 6:1-7 and Luke 16:19-31
preached at Grace Lutheran Church,
Green Bay, Wisconsin

The rich man wakes up. He's been having a nasty nightmare, one of those nightmares you consciously feel yourself trying to get out of, but nothing you see yourself doing in the nightmare ever works. It is one of those nightmares from which you awaken with the fear you felt in the midst of it still lingering in your mind.

The rich man rubs his eyes as if to wipe away the fearsome sights he'd seen in the nightmare. He's much consoled to look about his bright room that had a commanding view of the city and in which stood a massive bed of carved ivory. It's the Sabbath morning. Out of his strict adherence to the Law of Moses, his slaves rest on the Sabbath, but he'd been able to find many desperate people to work for money on the weekend to dress him in his fine Egyptian linens and purple robe and to wait on him as he feasted luxuriously so that he never had to lift a finger on the Sabbath, again, out of strict adherence to the Law of Moses.

The rich man is a Pharisee, a minority among those who worshiped the God of Israel in the time of Jesus. The Pharisees believed that God gave humankind rules for clean living, rules that included the Law of Moses, but also other rules based upon it. The rich man believed, as did most of his fellow Pharisees, that if you followed God's rules for clean living God blessed you; God blessed your every venture in life; God gave you sons and success in your vocation. And so it was. The rich man's father had had six sons and a successful business in which the rich man had shared and that the rich man had grown large enough so that his five brothers all lived quite comfortably.

People said to the rich man: "You must live right!"

After the rich man is dressed and has eaten, he leaves for the synagogue. At his gate, on this fine Sabbath morning, he finds only one beggar. The rich man did what he could for beggars. He had table scraps carried out to them. If they were able to walk, he sent them on errands and paid them for their efforts. But secretly, the rich man had thought of a way to discourage beggars from lounging around too long in front of his fine house. His gate faced south and bore the full blast of the desert sun. He refused to plant anything anywhere near the gate so that there was no shade in which beggars could idly lie; just gleaming, white hot stone, as hot as Hades. Eventually, the beggars who thought to try begging at his splendid house moved on unless they'd been thrown there and were unable to move, in which case ... well, you can imagine.

Beggars, the rich man thought, *are beggars for a reason.* To him their sicknesses, their disabilities, their drunkenness, their inability to manage to keep jobs — these were all signs of laziness, signs of sinfulness, and their miserable fate, therefore, was God's punishment. It clearly said in the Law of Moses, the book of Deuteronomy, chapter 28: "If you will not obey the Lord your God by diligently observing all his commandments and decrees ... then ... curses shall come upon you and overtake you" (Deuteronomy 28:15). However, "if you will only obey the Lord your God, by diligently observing all his commandments ... the Lord your God will set you high above all the nations of the earth; all these blessings shall come upon you and overtake you, if you obey the Lord your God" (Deuteronomy 28:1-2).

As a Pharisee the rich man diligently, scrupulously obeyed the Law of Moses and more, and he believed God had blessed him with prosperity, and so he truly felt unassailably blessed and good.

The beggar baking at his gate on this fine Sabbath morning is a particularly repulsive one, one with oozing sores the dogs seemed to like to lick. This beggar had been lying there all week too weak to walk, or even to shoo away the dogs that ate most of the food scraps before he could get to them.

The rich man slams his staff into the sides of several of the dogs that morning to keep them away from the beggar long enough so the beggar could eat. The rich man thinks he's excused for doing that bit of work on the Sabbath, because he'd done it to help another human being in distress.

The beggar, whose name the rich man had heard was Lazarus, thanks the rich man for his merciful generosity and reaches out to touch the rich man's robe. The rich man snatches his robes away, because if he were to have been touched by one who was so repulsively unclean, he would not be allowed to enter the synagogue without incurring the extra cost of ritual cleansing.

At synagogue, a guest teacher has come who the rich man dislikes the moment he sees him. The guest teacher looks as unkempt and suspicious as a beggar. Though the guest teacher reads well, he reads only from the prophets whom the rich man had always suspected were just angry and jealous men who couldn't hack a real job, who did nothing but complain about the government and who only wanted hard-working folks to feel bad about living a comfortable life. The rich man had secretly wondered if the other prophets whose writings did not make it into the scriptures had not written more beautiful and cheerful things. The guest teacher starts reading Amos:

> *Alas for those who are at ease in Zion, and for those who feel secure on Mount Samaria.*
>
> *Alas for those who lie on beds of ivory, and lounge on their couches ... who sing idle songs to the sound of the harp, and like David improvise on instruments of music; who drink wine from bowls, and anoint themselves with the finest oils, but are not grieved over the ruin of Joseph!*
>
> *Therefore they shall now be the first to go into exile, and the revelry of the loungers shall pass away.*
>
> — Amos 6:1, 4-7

The guest teacher rolls up the scroll and begins urging the Pharisees to sell all their possessions and follow him, because it's impossible to serve God and wealth. A good deal of grumbling and snorting goes on as the guest teacher speaks, and no one gets up and follows him as he leaves the synagogue during the closing announcements about the changes to the harp improvisation schedule for the week.

Upon his return home, the rich man notices that his paid staff are shoveling up the remains of the beggar named Lazarus. The rich man points to the little puddles of bodily fluids left behind and commands that they, too, be cleaned away following all the regulations for the elimiantion of biohazards. As the rich man steps beneath his splendid arched gateway he promptly collapses.

After having plummeted down to the fiery pit of Hades the rich man rubs his eyes, looks down at his ruined linens and purple robe, and wonders if this might be a nightmare. The rich man lifts up his eyes and sees Father Abraham far away, with that filthy beggar Lazarus at his side. *This is impossible!* the rich man thinks to himself. *This must be a mistake! That beggar was a sinner; he'd never been to synagogue! That beggar had never obeyed even half the laws of Moses I have! That beggar was a sinner and his misfortunes in life were God's punishments that are supposed to go on forever. Me ... out of strict adherence to the Law of Moses, I gave ten percent of my income faithfully my whole life long and now I'm burning in hell? It makes no sense!*

The rich man begs for mercy to his Father Abraham. He begs his Father Abraham to send Lazarus back to witness to his five brothers so that they don't end up in Hades.

Father Abraham's responses are not comforting. Father Abraham says that the rich man's brothers already have Moses and the prophets. The rich man quickly interjects that Moses and the prophets won't do any good for his brothers, but that maybe some spectacular miracle would help. "Maybe," says the rich man, "if someone returns to them from the dead! Like, like *me* maybe...."

Abraham thinks not.

A few weeks later, the rich man sees a man approaching him through the flames, approaching with a great crowd of people behind him. As the man gets closer, the rich man notices that he barely has any clothes on at all and that he's been beaten and gashed and that he's bleeding and, from the looks of his ankles and wrists, it appears as if he'd been crucified by the Romans as a criminal of some sort. The rich man is quite sure that this is a gang of thugs about to come to beat him, when he recognizes the man as the guest teacher in the synagogue who had indeed, suffered under

100

Pontius Pilate, was crucified, died, was buried, and had descended into hell.

The guest teacher, beaten and bedraggled and wretched as he is, reaches out to touch the rich man, who draws back. The guest teacher speaks: "You are forgiven."

"Forgiven?" shouts the rich man. "*I* am forgiven? Forgiven for what? And who are *you* to forgive sins? You're nothing but a common criminal! Who forgives sins but God alone? And in my book right now, *God* is the one who needs forgiveness, not me, because I have followed God's law to a tee to earn my everlasting reward and then I get this?"

The guest speaker replied, "Isn't it silly to imagine you could somehow have done enough to earn the unimaginably miraculous gift of everlasting life? The law is good, but not that good. The law is good, but it obviously hasn't made you good. Have you really loved your neighbor Lazarus as much as you loved yourself? Weren't you eager to separate yourself from him and those like him and their depressing diseases and hunger? You wanted only to be cheerful and secure. Didn't you refuse to plant trees before your gate so that those like Lazarus would be discouraged from begging there?"

"How do you know what I think?" objects the rich man.

"Say it isn't so," the guest teacher replies.

The rich man is silent.

The teacher gently persists, "Is such a trick truly the sign of a good man?"

The rich man is silent.

"You tried to isolate yourself from the plight of the poor; it was as if you tried put an ocean around yourself; and though your actions were always quite legal, were they and your thoughts really profoundly moral?"

"No," the rich man finally, begrudgingly admits.

"Then," Jesus says, again reaching out his filthy hand with its oozing, gaping sore, "that you may know that it is by the grace of God that you are saved, accept the forgiveness and welcome I have lived and died to proclaim: accept my forgiveness for your eagerness to be rid of all thoughts of the poor among you; accept my

101

forgiveness for your eagerness to always feel you were right and good on your own terms and not on the terms of Moses and the prophets."

The rich man looked at Jesus for a long, long time.

One wonders how you will respond.

Chapter Notes

1. David Buttrick, *Homiletic* (Philadelphia: Fortress Press, 1987), p. 334.

2. The phrase "willing suspension of disbelief" comes from Samuel Taylor Coleridge's "Biographia Literaria." In the midst of this piece of literary criticism, Coleridge describes how he and William Wordsworth came up with their two divergent approaches toward writing poetry. Where Wordsworth wanted to write poems that gave "charm of novelty to things of every day," Coleridge wanted to write poems in which "the incidents and agents were ... in part at least, supernatural." Coleridge did not limit the meaning of "supernatural" only to "incidents and agents" that were "divine," but also included "incidents and agents" that were not found in the "real world." The challenge of composing works using supernatural incidents and agents was to attempt to "transfer from our inward nature a human interest and semblance of truth sufficient to procure for these shadows of imagination that willing suspension of disbelief for the moment, which constitutes poetic faith." For Coleridge, transferring "human interest" from "our inward nature" to these kinds of fictional incidents and agents caused readers to "suspend their disbelief" that such incidents and agents were merely fictional. Without "poetic faith," presumably such fictional incidents and agents were in danger of being dismissed and of having no significant message to impart. Just so, the poetic license demanded by preaching by retelling or dramatizing biblical stories, demands a similar transfer of "human interest" from "our inward nature" to keep listeners/viewers from dismissing such stories as if they had no significant message to impart. Samuel Taylor Coleridge, "Biographia Literaria," comp. and eds James Harry Smith and Edd Winfield Parks, *The Great Critics*, 3d ed. (New York: W. W. Norton and Co., Inc., 1967), pp. 526-527.

3. Richard Jensen, *Thinking In Story* (Lima, Ohio: CSS Publishing Company, 1993), pp. 71-72, 76.

4. Another significant form of preaching less oriented toward developing a conventional plot is modeled on the forms of storytelling in the Old Testament. According to Jensen in *Thinking In Story,* storytelling in the Old Testament, true to its oral roots, is more episodic, less focused on achieving a chronologically oriented plot. Jensen uses Garrison Keillor's storytelling as a modern example of episodic storytelling, of "stitching stories together." The structure of such a sermon depends upon the idea of a "living center," a different perspective of which each of the stories stitched together reveals. Jensen refers readers to Eugene Lowry's book, *How to Preach a Parable: Designs for Narrative Sermons.* In this book Lowry describes several patterns by which to stitch biblical stories together with stories from real life in a sequence

based on conventional story plots. Jensen, *Thinking In Story*, pp. 23-24; 121-138.

5. I'm using the word myth as it is used in Herbert Anderson and Edward Foley, *Mighty Stories, Dangerous Rituals* (San Francisco: Jossey-Bass Publishers, 1998), pp. 12-16.

6. Anderson and Foley, pp. 12-16; John Dominic Crossan, *The Dark Interval* (Niles, Illinois: Argus Communications, 1975), p. 59.

7. Jana Childers, *Performing the Word: Preaching as Theatre* (Nashville: Abingdon Press, 1998), p. 96. See also Jensen, *Thinking*, and Henry Mitchell, *Celebration and Experience in Preaching* (Nashville: Abingdon Press, 1990), p. 44.

8. Childers, pp. 37-39. See also Richard Jensen, *Telling the Story* (Minneapolis: Fortress Press, 1980), pp. 138-144; Jensen, *Thinking*, p. 115.

9. Mitchell, p. 80.

10. Mitchell, p. 81.

11. Jensen, *Thinking*, pp. 20-21; Thomas Troeger, *Ten Strategies for Preaching in a MultiMedia Culture* (Nashville: Abingdon Press, 1996), p. 18.

12. Lucy Lind Hogan and Robert Reid, *Connecting with the Congregation: Rhetoric and the Art of Preaching* (Nashville: Abingdon Press, 1999), pp. 47-67; Katie Day, *Difficult Conversations* (Baltimore: The Alban Institute, 2001), pp. 29-41.

Chapter 6

I Just Can't Listen Unless There's Something Happening!

**Including Visual And Musical Dimensions
In Sermons Which Retell Biblical Stories**

The title of this chapter is a telling quote from a high school student. We preach to a people whose senses are attuned to, and hungry for, spectacular, multimedia stories. We live in a culture in which our oral-verbal attention span is about a sound bite long. Life has a soundtrack. "We live in an age of polymorphic massages of our senses."[1] We can't listen unless something is happening. In order to communicate *at all*, therefore, it's obvious that we preachers have to start engaging our listeners/viewers in new ways. I have found that my specific methodology for retelling or dramatizing biblical stories is one of those ways. Even the simplest forms of dramatizations engage listeners/viewers visually. Clark, a member of one of my preaching groups, commented favorably about the level of visual suspense generated by one of my project sermons. The sermon kept him wondering, "Who's going to pop out next?" Another telling story: the stewardship board that I presently serve produced a video about the ways that members of the congregation serve others through the ministries of our congregation. Although there were three high school students in the videotape, *everyone else* was at least forty years old; most were much older. Yet at the 8 a.m. Sunday service, I watched a fourteen-year-old boy who was serving as an acolyte (usually barely conscious at that hour) absolutely transfixed by these stories about how and why a bunch of middle-aged and old people participated in the ministries of our congregation. All this without one single special effect!

Spectacle

Actually, compared to worship, even with all their special effects, the power of movies to move people is limited. Because

105

sermons are embedded in worship that can be alive with the energy of many kinds of participants, sermons have a potential element of interactivity at a level greater than most media. (If we could figure out how to work a mouse or a joystick into worship, the sky would be the limit!) In his book, *The Spectacle of Worship in a Wired World*, Tex Sample envisions a form of worship analogous to a cultural phenomenon he calls "spectacle." Sample (and others) believe we live in an "electronic culture," and that for people living in an electronic culture "bonding and commitment" most readily occur in events called "spectacles." Spectacles are events in which there is a "convergence of ... sensory experiences."[2] Summarizing the insights of other students of the electronic culture, Sample thinks that for those people living in it "meaning is conveyed through experience."[3] Spectacles can be popular music concerts, sports competitions, musicals or opera, or even a worship service. What stories spectacles tell will vary. When spectacles don't tell stories that inspire people to engage in creating a sense of community or fulfill a particular mission, Sample thinks spectacles create "publics" — individuals who make up a market niche or a fan-base.[4] A market niche is not a community like the living Body of Christ that Paul envisions (Romans 12:4-7 or 1 Corinthians 12:4-31). But because spectacle *can* unite people and convey meaning for members of the electronic culture, it is important to continue to develop ways to use spectacle to tell *our* story, the gospel. We can do this by adding music and drama to the retelling of biblical stories in many different ways. We'll discuss a few ways to do this in a moment.

David Buttrick, in *Homiletic*, is concerned about sermons that contain elements of spectacle. He regards them primarily as "performances." He claims that they result in listeners/viewers taking away only individualized ideas about the meaning of the event. For Buttrick, "Rightly, preaching is a conversation with a congregation. By addressing people, preaching draws a congregation into one consciousness; it unifies."[5] Performances, according to Buttrick, drive people into "personal subjectivity" and "lock people into their own affective responses" and "do not belong in the pulpit as part of public worship."[6] According to Sample, however, in spectacles, people are definitely not "locked" into their own affective responses; they are linked to each other by their common, emotional experience.[7] Jana Childers, in her book, *Performing the Word*, draws specific parallels between preaching and dramatic performance and affirms that preaching has "the power to create community and communion by drawing people together in a common purpose."[8] Who is right? Short of using worship as a context for a sociological study, neither "side" can know for sure. It's hard to ignore the evidence of Sample and others that an epistemological revolution is in progress. What if the Reformers had ignored the printing press?

I'd Like To Teach The World To Sing

Music is ideally suited to story *and* to reaching and uniting the hearts and souls of listeners/viewers. Once I heard a radio broadcast that convinced me of this in a particularly moving way. During the broadcast, writer Anne Lamott told a story about an event that occurred during a worship service in her church.[9] During the service, the congregation was about to sing a hymn and so, in her story, Lamott described how the pianist began to introduce the hymn. As Lamott told this part of the story during the radio broadcast, a pianist began to play on the radio broadcast an introduction to the same hymn the congregation sang in Lamott's story. At the very moment the pianist began to play, I felt drawn into the story Lamott was telling so intensely that I began to see the setting of the story and the faces and actions of the main characters. It was an amazing experience. When Lamott described how the main character made a surprising gesture of compassion, I felt a profound sense of joy that the gospel had been done; I felt that joy as intensely as if I had been sitting right there in Lamott's church. It brought tears to my eyes. *Jesus lives!* is what I was thinking and feeling. There was no sense that the story was meant to elicit a hundred individualized points of view about what was happening any more than the stories Jesus told did.[10] All listeners were invited to rejoice together about the way the main character acted out the gospel. The musical accompaniment of the story immediately helped draw me, all of me, the thinking *and* feeling me, deeply into the story.

I'm quite sure I wasn't the only one to respond in this way. I borrowed the core event of Lamott's story to use in a sermon for Reformation Sunday. I retold the story in my own words related to a particular lesson (not part of Lamott's story at all), and used the piano music to draw people deeply into the story. Many people told me they responded just as I had to the story I heard on the radio. Together, many people wept for joy when they heard and saw the gospel done by the main character of the story. The sermon, which concludes this chapter, was a spectacle. The sermon became an event that invited us to believe in the presence of God in that story and among us. This was most certainly "a performance," and though it may very well have led many to reflect individually on the meaning of the event, many people celebrated it *together* as well. As Henry Mitchell puts it: "people recall far better what they have celebrated well"[11] and "people *do* what they celebrate."[12] We *do* want people to remember and to *do* the gospel, so that our story makes a bigger impact on the world around us than even the most frenetic and ambitious multi-media spectaculars. In this way, I think music can be a catalyst, a way of stirring up our souls, so that we can seek and grasp and celebrate the gospel. While Barbara Brown Taylor despairs of the preacher's ability to use "soiled, tired language" to "do justice to the Word," she believes that "God remains among us as music" (and that "the Holy Spirit is the breath that brings both word and music to life").[13]

Well-chosen hymns that echo the message of the sermon are also vital. When people are surprised to hear echoes of the sermon in the hymns, they often have a sense of the Spirit having been active in the course of worship to reveal a message especially to them.[14] Some, or all, of the verses from these hymns that particularly echo the message of sermons can be sung or quoted by the preacher in the midst of sermons; some, or all, of the verses can be sung by the congregation after the sermon ends. In effect, then, congregations can *sing* the sermon together, not just simply be *addressed* by the pastor. This practice is apparently "old hat" for the African-American preaching tradition as Henry Mitchell reports:

108

"Great hymns of the church ... have the advantage of being familiar and of offering a means of congregational participation in the celebration, since they may be sung just after they have been recited [as part of a sermon]. There is always the temptation to use them too often, but in moderation they are marvelous vehicles of celebration which involve the entire congregation."[15]

I also find that the prayers in liturgical resources almost always lift up a theme or a message I aimed at in the sermon. Sometimes I'll use a word, or an image or two, from the sermon to modify the prayers to make the sermon's message echo more clearly in them, to make the sermon's message something listeners/viewers also pray to God to fulfill in their lives. Congregations can *pray* sermons together as well. That sermons including music are performances in some ways and that people come away with individualized understandings of it are all very likely true as Buttrick charges. Preachers can easily avoid Buttrick's concerns about this if they reinforce the message of the sermon again and again throughout the rest of the worship service.

The True Enchantment Of Story

Finally, maybe stories themselves are a form of music, a form of enchantment. One member of my preaching group objected to the rest of the group's idea that I start summarizing the messages of my story sermons in a few well-chosen words for people who might have been having trouble understanding them. Her objection implies she felt a profound difference between mere words and a story: "I don't think [you should provide summaries]. You're using a story, then you switch back to words." Stories, it has long been believed, have the power to suspend our disbelief. Adding visual excitement and music to stories can only increase this power. I used to think it would be silly to imagine we could compete with Hollywood's multimedia, multi-million dollar spectaculars. But in a way, we Christians have the advantage even without the budget and the technology. Hollywood's stories just show up on big screens in big dark rooms or on little glass screens in front of which individuals hunch. We believe our spectacles are about the truth; in worship we can celebrate, sing, and pray the truth *together*. And when our spectacles are over, we don't just go home; we continue to meet together, to talk together, to work together to live out our stories individually and corporately. We believe our spectacles can transform random gatherings of people into the living, breathing, acting Body of Christ. Our stories can be sacramental. Hollywood's stories are famous for fifteen minutes or maybe fifteen days or at most, fifteen months. Our stories will go on to the very end of the age, because our stories are the truth. How much more then, should we use every engaging communication method our culture has devised when we preachers attempt to proclaim the truth, especially when we proclaim it in tales twice told?

* * *

I Sing Because I'm Free
A Sermon for Reformation Sunday
(Revised Common Lectionary, Cycle A)
based on Romans 3:19-28
preached at Grace Lutheran Church,
Green Bay, Wisconsin

Maria had grown up Catholic. Maria knew what was what. She knew where you're supposed to be every Sunday morning. She liked Sunday morning. She went with her mother and her aunt to church on Sunday morning. She loved the church because it was beautiful, so beautiful and clean compared to the hot, stuffy, pink cinder block apartment building she lived in off a dirty, treeless alley in Los Angeles.

One entered Maria's church through an arch in a towering white adobe wall, on a white stone path that led through a tropical garden courtyard with colorful parrots squawking in the boughs of trees blossoming with orange or purple flowers. In the narthex, Maria met colorful statues of saints standing beside the still waters of a cool baptismal pool at the entrance to the high-ceilinged nave in which tall, colorful windows cast rainbows down through the dust onto the people. The priest, dressed in colorful robes — red and purple and gold — was like one of the statues of the saints come alive; he was constantly flanked by white-robed attendants. Maria loved when the priest held up the round white host at communion, when he held it high up so she could see the glorious gleaming marble of the body of Jesus on the cross behind the bread. Maria loved the church and its beauty and its music and was proud to be there at her mother's side. She was dutiful to the laws of the church and to her mother. Her mother greatly appreciated this one daughter of hers who obeyed and gave her no trouble — the daughter who shouldered much of the mothering chores, who marched her little brothers around, and kept their white shirts clean and ironed for church and school.

But as her little brothers grew older, they learned that girls were only beautiful objects to impress and pursue and to give them pleasure. They learned that girls would be impressed by bravado, by nice abs and many points scored in a game. They found much of this true among girls of their own age, but they found that none of it impressed their older sister Maria. They could lift weights until they were shiny bronze gods and boast about smoking cigarettes and drinking, and though all these things impressed girls their age, they did not impress Maria in the least. They would walk around bare-chested, smoking cigarettes, and flexing their pectorals, and Maria would laugh at them and call them babies and tell them that unless they did their schoolwork, they'd just get fat and sick and work at Burrito Bell the rest of their lives.

Deep, deep down Maria's brothers knew she was right, but they hated school, and not one of them wanted to stand up to those who taught them to hate school. Deep, deep down they did know the path they were on — headed nowhere, and rather than admit that to their big sister, they scorned her and made fun of her, called her Santa Maria, Mother of God.

Maria steeled herself against this treatment of her brothers, graduated from high school, earned an associate degree, got a job as a dental hygienist, worked her way out of the barrio, married, and followed her husband's career to San Francisco. There she joined her husband's Presbyterian church, because it was a beautiful place as the church had been in her childhood. There she was invited to wear the silky robes of the choir which sang exquisite,

111

holy music in an exquisite, holy space. Maria sang with great pride overflowing in her heart. She sang looking down on the congregation, looking down on her husband and her two beautiful boys in their white shirts. She sang proudly with tears in her eyes, because she believed her efforts had been rewarded, because she was justified in believing her obedience and good works could free her from the barrio, because she believed she was justified in thinking her obedience and good works would earn her the blessings of her beautiful home and her beautiful husband and her two beautiful boys. All that Maria had achieved was beautiful, good, righteous, holy, except for one thing: a man who began coming to church and sitting in a front pew.

He was a thin man. A pale man. Thin and pale as a skeleton. His arms were bones sticking out of big sleeves of old wrinkled, short-sleeved dress shirts. Sometimes this man fell asleep in church, actually just laid down in the pew. A lot of weeks, he never even bothered to show up. After a time, this man even had the audacity to wheel an IV stand down the aisle with him.

"Right into church he brought that thing," Maria complained to a fellow choir member. "I don't know why he comes," Maria went on, "most of the time he just comes and sleeps and you know he's one of them; you know he's got AIDS."

Just the thought of a man with AIDS sent shivers down Maria's spine. *What those men do*, Maria thought with horror and disgust, *and then they come to church to flaunt their diseases.* Maria was raised Catholic. She knew what was what. She knew that man was disobeying God's law and should not be in church. But he really irked her when he began coming with his ... friend ... and when the two of them sat there in the front row in front of God and everybody leaning on each other.

She complained to the pastor. She railed about it to her husband. She sliced and diced those two with bitter humor with her friends in choir. But during church, up in the choir risers, her heart burned with indignation that they would come and desecrate God's house with their presence and disobedience. *He's ruining everything*, she thought, *ruining everything, making me so angry.*

Maria could not free herself from these feelings.

112

So she was happy when for a long time he didn't show up. She felt free of her anxiety about this man, free of her anger, free of her choked-up frustration with him and his kind. But he came back. Alone.

He clung to the pew ends, staggered down the aisle alone, and he just laid down in the front pew. He didn't even try to sit up. It was the hymn after the sermon. *(Accompanist begins playing an introduction to "His Eye Is On The Sparrow," preferably on the piano.)* And Maria was watching him. He seemed to stir suddenly upon hearing the introduction to the hymn and Maria saw him reaching for the hymnal and paging through the hymnal desperately, pathetically, because just as he seemed to have reached the page, the pages slipped out of his hands. The hymnal slipped off the pew and fell to the floor with an annoying clunk, but immediately he was reaching for it again, reaching frantically for it and finding it and picking it up by the cover *(ruining the binding,* Maria was thinking in disgust) and putting it in front of his face again as he lay there in the pew just as the congregation rose up and began to sing:

(Preacher or soloist sings.)

> *Why should I feel discouraged?*
> *Why should the shadows come?*
> *Why should my heart be lonely*
> *And long for heav'n and home*
> *When Jesus is my portion? My constant Friend is he;*
> *His eye is on the sparrow*
> *And I know He watches me;*
> *His eye is on the sparrow,*
> *And I know He watches me.*[16]

(Accompanist plays another verse of "His Eye Is On The Sparrow" concluding the sermon with the refrain.)

Maria watched the man as she sang and she saw that he was hanging on to his hymnal so desperately his arm was trembling. Then she saw his lips moving, and she saw him singing. She saw

113

the hymnal slipping away again, she saw tears flowing down his face, and she saw the hymnal drop to the floor again. For some reason she could not understand, under the influence of some power she could not comprehend, she closed her own hymnal and rushed down to the man and knelt beside him. She picked up his hymnal and picked up his bony, bony body and put her arm around him so he could lean on her, she opened the hymnal. She held the hymnal and he turned the pages and there were lines left for them to sing together:

(Preacher or soloist sings.)

> *I sing because I'm happy, I sing because I'm free*
> *For His eye is on the sparrow*
> *And I know He watches me.*[17]

Amen.

Chapter Notes

1. Richard Jensen, *Thinking In Story* (Lima, Ohio: CSS Publishing Company, 1993), pp. 47, 142; Henry Mitchell, *Celebration and Experience in Preaching* (Nashville: Abingdon Press, 1990), p. 17; Tex Sample, *The Spectacle of Worship in a Wired World* (Nashville: Abingdon Press, 1998), pp. 76-94.

2. Sample, p. 78.

3. Sample, pp. 89-91.

4. Sample, p. 92.

5. David Buttrick, *Homiletic* (Philadelphia: Fortress Press, 1987), p. 334.

6. Buttrick, p. 334.

7. Sample, p. 57.

8. Jana Childers, *Performing the Word: Preaching as Theatre* (Nashville: Abingdon Press, 1998), p. 37.

9. The story originally appeared in Anne Lamott, *Traveling Mercies: Some Thoughts about Faith* (New York: Pantheon Books, 1999), pp. 63-65.

10. In the first chapter of his book, *Hear Then the Parable*, Bernard Brandon Scott discusses at length the *limitation* of the scope of meaning for a parable: "Narrative becomes parable when it enters into the kingdom's field of reference. A hearer confronts simultaneously story and expectations implied in the kingdom of God, expectations drawn from the religious heritage's repertoire. Just as a hearer must make sense of the story, so, also, he or she must make sense of the relation between story (discourse) and the kingdom." I think congregations hearing sermons are in a rhetorical context comparable to original hearers of parables. The question that faces almost any listener/viewer during a sermon is "What does this scripture have to do with my life?" This question limits the amount of possible meanings discerned in a story sermon in a way different from a theatrical performance in which no such limiting question governs the listeners/viewers expectations. Bernard Brandon Scott, *Hear Then the Parable* (Minneapolis: Fortress Press, 1989), p. 62.

11. Mitchell, p. 30.

12. Mitchell, p. 62.

13. Barbara Brown Taylor, *When God is Silent* (Cambridge, Massachusetts: Cowley Publications, 1998), pp. 120, 119.

14. Don E. Saliers, *Worship as Theology: Foretaste of the Glory Divine* (Nashville: Abingdon Press, 1994), p. 23; Sample, p. 95.

15. Mitchell, pp. 70, 68.

16. The text for this hymn is public domain.

17. The text for this hymn is public domain.

Epilogue

Confession is good for the soul. It's about telling the truth. One of the requirements of the Doctor of Ministry process with which I never complied was developing a "Sermon Purpose Statement" *before* writing my sermons. We were supposed to have written this statement even before discussing the sermon texts with our preaching groups. If I had already settled on a purpose for the sermon before discussing the lessons with the group, I'm not sure that their participation in preparing the sermon would have been so profoundly helpful for me. As I have noted, several ideas, even entire *lines* in the sermons came directly from the members of the preaching groups! My objection to Sermon Purpose Statements went deeper than this obvious problem. It had to do with the creative processes of character and plot development described in this book. If you set a character free to live, breathe, speak, and act in and beyond the boundaries of a pericope, you'll enjoy some homiletical surprises no Sermon Purpose Statement could anticipate.

It is important, however, *after* your is sermon is complete, to imagine yourself as the listener/viewer (one perhaps, who has to fill out a Sermon Notes form for Confirmation!) and try to summarize the point of your sermon in one sentence. There are several reasons why coming up with a Sermon Purpose Statement after you're done writing is a good discipline. When the rhetorical effect you are trying to achieve depends upon connecting with a biblical character and not upon a clearly defined set of didactic points, listeners/viewers can get stuck in a personal connection they've made with the story that may be tangential to your purpose. Analyzing everything you fabricate and create about your characters in light of a Sermon Purpose Statement will help minimalize this kind of confusion. Every word and detail must point steadfastly in one direction. Secondly, caught up in the excitement of your creativity you might inadvertently forget or modify a salient detail in a pericope. People may notice these differences between the pericope and your story. When they do, they can be distracted by suspicions about why you're distorting the pericope and the spell of willing suspension of disbelief is broken.

Finally, these kinds of sermons *do* demand more of listeners/ viewers. People who like to understand things through logical presentations which analyze and elucidate ideas in clear, step-by-step processes, may be frustrated and confused having to examine feelings and questions left by some stories. Once my daughter wrote a story with a strange, inscrutable ending for her middle school writing teacher whose primary teaching expertise was science. The main character in my daughter's story was a girl who had found what she believed to be a valuable gold coin in the ocean. Several people ridiculed the girl for believing the coin was real. Without telling us why, the narrator concludes the story rather abruptly by describing how the girl throws the coin back into the ocean. Up to this point, the reader feels there's enough evidence to justify the girl's pursuit of more research about the coin, so the reader is confused and perhaps even angry with the girl for tossing a potentially valuable coin back into the sea. To a scientifically-oriented teacher expecting a nice logical, realistic plot, the story seemed to be capricious nonsense and was graded likewise. Upon first reading it, I too, was angry with the girl in the story; I too, felt the ending was capricious nonsense, until I thought more about my feelings toward the girl and questioned more deeply why she'd thrown the coin away. Maybe it was that she valued her own faith in the coin, and she could not bear to have it mocked. Maybe throwing it into the sea was a way of protecting what she felt was valuable. Maybe the story is a parable about faith in a cynical world, a world not inclined to help its young people explore faith, but simply to discount it, ignore it, overwhelm it with a million multimedia spectacles. Or maybe it was a story about the fearfulness of examining one's faith; maybe something or someone *could* prove that faith is unfounded. Maybe the story expressed both sets of thoughts and feelings at once. In order to understand *any* story, readers or hearers must be encouraged to linger over it a bit, reflecting upon the thoughts and feelings the story raises up in them.

Several times in the course of my studies, I've been encouraged to write a little summary of my sermon in the bulletin for folks who have trouble understanding story sermons. Richard Jensen quotes Flannery O'Connor who gives us the quintessential response to such requests: "People have a habit of saying, 'What is the theme of your story?' and they expect you to give them a statement: 'The theme of my story is the economic pressure of the machine on the middle class' — or some such absurdity. When they have got a statement like that, they go off happy and feel it is no longer necessary to read the story."[1] I have never provided such summaries. There is, however, at least one way I have found to suggest a question or a theme to listen for during my sermons. I do this during the children's message that comes right before the sermon. These suggestions can guide both children and adults as they reflect on the questions that may be raised for them as I retell a biblical story.

The best way to help those confused by story sermons is to invite people to talk about your sermons with you. This is what my preaching groups did after each parish project sermon. Sometimes we invited the whole congregation into this conversation. Your openness to discussing your sermons will go a long way to helping people accept and enjoy new forms of preaching. In larger congregations, offering opportunities to discuss your sermon immediately following the sermon is sometimes logistically problematic. Offer the opportunity anyway, even if it's later in the day, especially if you *are* concerned about people feeling confused, especially if you are just beginning to preach by retelling biblical stories. These sessions will be filled with hours of teachable moments for your members and for yourself. You will be surprised by what people hear. Sometimes you'll be dismayed. You'll always learn something about the scriptures, about how people experience sermons (of any kind), and about the art of preaching by telling stories. The extra effort is worth it, because, after all, they're not *just* stories you're telling; you're telling the truth! And the truth deserves our best.

Chapter Notes

1. Flannery O'Conner, *Mystery and Manners*, eds. Sally and Robert Fitzgerald (New York: Farrar, Straus, Giroux, 1969), p. 73.